MAKE HER BEG FOR YOU

SECRETS OF A MASTER SEDUCER ON HOW TO ATTRACT WOMEN

by Andy Soraklis

CONTENTS

ABOUT THE AUTHOR

Andy Soraklis is a 35 year old life coach, personal trainer, software engineer and entrepreneur who lives in New York. He has met with more than 10000 women to sleep with more than 50 to ultimately love 1. He currently actively meets with women, runs bethabit.com, writes books and invests in real estate. He strictly believes that every man must have a purpose in life rather than chasing women and every man must use his raw sexual desire to get whatever he wants in life.

INTRODUCTION

The problem with most dating and relationship advice today is that they all sell the same bullshit marketing message of "do this and get laid today" or "just be confident" cliche to make a boring fat guy to believe he can have sex with a model if he has sufficient "game" or "confidence".

They make guys think that a system of stories, routines and mindsets are going to trick a high quality woman into bed, and keep her around.

I was the guy who was getting high quality women into my bed from time to time but there was a big fact I knew; it was simple but never easy.

If it was easy, humanity would never advance, capitalism would collapse, no man would buy fast cars and build empires. But we still like to hear "the one easy step" right?

There is a famous quote of an Indian Chief that goes like this:

Indian Chief was asked by a white government official... "You have observed the white man for 90 years. You've seen his wars and his technological advances. You've seen his progress, and the damage he's done...Considering all these events, in your opinion, where did the white man go wrong?"

The chief stared at the government official for a long time

and then calmly replied. "When white man find land, Indians running it. No taxes, No debt, Plenty buffalo, Plenty beaver, Clean Water; Women did all the work, Medicine man free. Indian man spend all day hunting and fishing; All night having sex with multiple women."

Then the chief leaned back and smiled. "Only white man is dumb enough to think that he can improve a system like that."

The American Indians lived in that land for thousands of years with no advancement. When the White Man came (with his sexual energy monogamously focused and directed) he found the Indian still living in tents, not wearing clothing, shitting in the forest, and living like savages. However, they were having unlimited amount of sex.

Wouldn't you live in middle of nowhere like a savage if you knew you wouldn't work for money and you would have sex with multiple women everyday? I would. And I would not care about a single thing in the world.

A sexually open society is a society that cannot survive the long term. If you disagree maybe you can ask an American Indian. What's that, can't find an American Indian to ask?

Every time you drive your car, use a toilet, cook your food on a stove, turn on the air conditioner or get food out of your refrigerator; you are actually enjoying the benefits of a man who used his sexual energy in a productive way, because he wanted to sleep with a hot woman just like you want now.

So, in this society, it can't be easy. It's simple when you take consistent action to find a woman who matches your energy, but it will never be easy. If it was easy, society would collapse. If it was easy, everyone would do it. Monogamy is the foundation of capitalism.

I was so pissed off to those people who were selling the dream, I knew if I wrote a book about it, it would never sell. How can you sell hard work? Hard work in any case. If you won't build your business to make a hot woman to choose you, then you will get rejected thousands of times to make that hot woman to choose you. Two different ways, same ending. In both cases, it's fucking hard work and nothing else.

This book is dedicated to the love of my life I had to lose. She said that I must write my experiences and when I remember her, she actually never wanted anything else from me. This book is my accountability to her and I really don't care if it sells or not.

I started by talking about the pickup and dating industry. I want to tell you the problem of it.

So people really buy products of these "gurus". Don't get me wrong, some of them are really solid guys. They have most probably said what I'm going to say in this book. The fact is though; people perfectly learn the theory from them. When it comes to application, they get stuck in anxiety and fear. What they learn is no different than learning how to get rich from a book. Most of them quit without even properly trying.

Some of these guys go further though. They hire dating coaches or go to bootcamps. This way of learning helps for sure because they get pushed to meet with women. However, coaches charge very high amounts of fees. An average earning guy can afford just 1 or 2 days of a coach or a bootcamp. When the coaching session ends, the guy is alone with himself to quickly to find out that the anxiety he used to have is still there as before. Now, he begins to look deeper.

This book is designed to solve the problems of that guy who looks deeper.

This isn't one of those training programs or books that throws a bunch of game or dating theory at you, pumps you up and then leaves you alone. This book is a 28 day intensive hands-on book that is designed to make meeting any women any time anywhere a habit ingrained in your nervous system.

You have to be eager to change yourself though. If you think you will manifest some pussy sitting on the couch without taking any action, please return this book back because it's not for you. I'm not a bullshitter and you will understand that as you read. The most important thing you can do is to take action and any experienced person would tell you that.

So let this book be your last book about this topic because you really have more important things to do in life rather than learning how to attract women. Go after your purpose and succeed so women will choose you anyway. If you are on your way to achieve your purpose, then go after women to find the right one(s) by systemizing the process to spend least time and emotions on it.

What you need is already inside you, hidden in your natural sexuality. You really, really won't need any more information than what I will write here in this book.

First and most important, this book will teach you how you can cultivate and project your raw sexual desire. Then, it will give you actionable theory that is based on my structured and tested open & escalate model. Third, it will present you powerful solutions to make you meet with women daily. Lastly; it will change the way you see meeting with women from the pain of failure to pleasure of success.

I promise you, if you take action, at the end of these 28 days, meeting any women any time any where will be your daily habit. You will also find out that after doing 500 approaches, at least one of the women will be yours regardless of your circumstances.

Open and Escalate Model

It is so important to have a structure in your interactions with women. Because if you are new to meeting with women, you will suck at it. You won't know what to do, your interactions won't go well, you won't know what you are doing.

If you have a structure though, you will know what you are doing, where you are and you will be in control. You will go each interaction confidently knowing what to do and how to lead her. Having a structure will give you strength, relaxation and comfort.

Open and escalate model is a structure that I developed through my experiences and being inspired by various seduction models. Unlike traditional dating and pickup advice though, it is not based on game, routines, frames of mind, confidence, tactics or techniques. It is based on developing your raw sexual desire and projecting that desire to a woman in a structure.

Human beings have different parts in their brain stacked on top of each other. If we were to split up your interaction with a woman, there are three levels of interaction happening in lower, middle and higher parts of your brain.

The lower part, which is called the reptilian brain, is the most ancient and primitive part of your brain. It handles all basic biological functions like eating, breathing, moving, feeling hungry, seeking food, feeling horny and seeking sex. Your subconscious lies in your reptilian brain which has 40000 times more capacity than your conscious.

The middle part is our mammalian brain, which enables you to have feelings for relationships, sympathy and empathy. No living organism can match the social and emotional processing power of our mammalian brain.

The upper part of your brain is neocortex, that handles language, abstraction, planning, reasoning, and strategy. It allows us to process situations and get above the emotional fray to an extent that the other mammals largely cannot.

These brains stack one on top of the other, and <u>when there is a decision to be made the lower brain almost always wins</u>. That means that if you have a strong urge to eat food, you can try to will yourself away from it with neocortical reasoning. However at some point if the urge goes on long enough or you stay around temptation long enough, you burn through your willpower reserve and finally give in. That also means that if you have a fear of meeting women or problems with getting her to bed, trying to solve it by logical thinking won't take you far.

That's why when human beings secure sex (reproduction) through masturbation or an average mate; they tend to sit on the couch, not risking their comfort zones.

Logically, you may want a new mate, but biologically you won't act if you are satisfied. If your biology wants you to do something and your logic wants you to do something else, while your logic may win in the short term, your biology will eventually wear your logic out.

You have to want women more biologically than you logically want them. The solution is of course having a high sexual desire. However sometimes that's not even enough. Even when you want a new mate biologically by being horny, another biological imperative "the fear of failure" will challenge you.

The key lies in letting your sexuality override your logic as well as biological fear of failure. This is why I will repeat how important your sexual energy is over and over again in this book. This is why open-escalate model focuses on cultivating and projecting your "raw sexual desire" to her in a structured way.

Traditional pickup models focus on the upper part of the brain. It is the "what do I say" and "what do I do" level. The specific things of the interaction such as your opening line, dhvs, negs, conversation topics, body language and eye contact. You imitate the alpha man, memorize routines, patterns and pick up lines. You see meeting women as a game. If you play it right, you will indeed succeed.

Traditional dating advice focuses on middle mammalian brain. It is the "how you behave" and "who you are" level. It's the "be truly confident" advice. Most popular dating books almost always cover that. You become aware that the frame you adopt can change the meaning of what you say and also help you say the right things. You accept who you are and act according to the right frame of mind. If you know what you want and have a strong frame, you will indeed succeed.

Open-escalate model focuses on reptilian brain. It is the hard-coded primal level of communication that made caveman laid before spoken language evolved. It is how a man and a woman who can't speak the same language can still have sex. It is the level where sub-communications occur. It stems from both your and her primal desires and basic instincts. It doesn't care about what you talk, confidence, etc.

The words and the frame are considerably less important than the sub-communications that you give off to her reptilian brain. It is the level where you can sleep with her without doing or saying the right thing. Your sub-communications will transmit powerful masculine behaviors to her and she will pick up on it. It comes down to one most important thing. Raw Sexual Desire.

<u>The best way you can attract, seduce and sleep with a woman is to desire her genuinely.</u>

I am talking about the <u>raw sexual desire</u> that you feel in your blood and rock hard erected dick. I am talking about the sexual desire that is more overpowering than any negative emotion associated with your fears such as fear of failure, talking with her, approaching her, what others think, how rich you are, how good looking you are, how old you are or your social status.

I'm talking about the exact opposite of what traditional pickup and dating advice says. I say forget about being alpha or high status truly confident guy and desire her with no strings attached.

Your natural instincts I mean. Pure animal state. That raw feeling when you look at her that makes your body move. The raw sexual energy that you feel when you imagine how it would feel to see her fully naked, to see her lying on her back with her legs open, waiting for you to put your rock hard dick into her tight wet pussy.

The model takes this raw sexual desire as the foundation and builds upon it by two parts. Opening and escalation.

Opening part is making the women open to your sexual advances. First you build your sexual and playful vibe through your raw sexual desire and ability to get into the zone. Then you select your target according to what you desire in a woman, considering your DNA matching.

Then you approach massive amounts of women by time intervals, with clear direct sexual intent and knowing what you want. You deliver specific openers that you formulate according to how she makes you feel in that specific moment of time. When you find what you want, you will flirt with her without getting personal in the beginning. You will project your sexual and playful energy through flirting.

Then you start having a normal conversation. You get to know who she is and share about your authentic self. When you realise that you have a connection going on, you decrease your energy to make her invest in you. This means you opened the woman for your sexual advances and completed part one. Now you pass on to part two which is escalation.

In the escalation part; you now focus on verbally and physically escalating her to sex while while you are still flirting and having regular conversation. For example while you are getting to know her you will be playing with her hands and you will be teasing her by making sexual comments.

Escalation consists of light, medium and heavy verbal and physical escalation. Every step is based on her comfort level. You will increase the intimacy as she shows compliance. After heavy escalation you will sleep with her.

The order of actions you have to take is what makes the model so effective. When you apply open and escalate model, the whole energy of the seduction will change. It will cause a wide range of emotions and trust.

For example, in the opening part, after you approach a girl, if you start a regular conversation with her such as asking what she does, she won't be engaging properly. She will wonder who you are and ask herself why should she care about telling a stranger about herself and her life.

But when you flirt with the girl first, you will get her emotions going. If she will be attracted to you, it will happen in this phase. So when you do get to regular conversation she will be interested in telling herself so a connection between you and her will happen.

The order applies to escalation part too. If you start to sexualise her too soon without creating a connection, you will come across sleazy. By making sure you create a connection first and doing escalation according to her compliance levels; you will be in control of your and her sexual desire.

How to Use This Book

Make your mind to commit 28 days of approaching 500 women in a quite intensive fashion. Do your plans for the next 4 weeks accordingly. Don't bitch and complain that it's not possible in where you live, it's too much or you don't have time. You need to do it daily to make it a habit. I will present you 3 powerful ways to make yourself do it starting from day 1.

You will be meeting with women walking on the street in general. You can also meet in the bar, club, shopping centers, cafes, basically everywhere. I will show you how to do it on the street which is the hardest so everywhere else will be easy for you.

The book consists of theory and practice parts. The theory of the book consists of four main parts.

In the first week we will focus on getting into zone by accepting who you are. You will approach women with the sole aim of taking her home without knowing about the open escalate model because <u>you already have what you need</u>.

Second week we will focus on your raw sexual desire and how to project it to women.

Third week you will learn the opening part of the model. You will learn to approach right, formulate openers, create attraction and comfort.

Fourth week you will learn the escalation part. You will learn how to rapidly escalate women you meet to sex.

Practice part is you doing set number of approaches daily to do 500 in 28 days. You will burn the bridges and do them.

The book consists of chapters as days. I recommend you to read one chapter a day, right after you come home after meeting with women.

Get ready to commit tomorrow. We will be together for the next 28 days and I will share you all my experiences I accumulated to make you a better person.

DAY 1 - GET INTO THE ZONE | TRUST YOUR INSTINCTS

Why You Must Cold Approach

You will solely cold approach women in these 28 days. Before we talk about how you will do it, we should talk about why you must do it.

I know you don't want to be a "cold-approach weirdo". I know that there are so many people trying to lead you astray from cold approaching.

You may have heard many people say cold approaching is a waste of time or a female friend of yours may have told you that it's creepy. You may have tried it and came to the conclusion that it's weird or it doesn't work for you.

For any reason, if you have doubts about cold approaching, let me tell you this to clear all your doubts.

<u>Cold approaching is the single most effective and empowering thing you can learn to improve your sex life. It is so effective that few things in life will alter the direction of your sex life as profoundly as the ability to cold approach successfully.</u>

However, if cold approaching really is effective, why are so many forces trying to lead you astray? Why you don't see anyone on the street doing it? Why it seems so hard? why do people feel like a weirdo after doing that?

The answer is simple. If you would be annoyed with a homeless person asking you for money, an attractive woman is more likely to being annoyed about being hit for sex in the same context. And it's not wrong. However, it's missing one crucial part. <u>She is being approached by a man she doesn't like.</u>

Imagine an attractive woman wearing a tight summer dress and walks down the street. All men she passes notice her, and she knows that they all want to sleep with her. Suddenly, a guy stops her and tells "Excuse me..I saw you walking here and I had to come and tell you that you have the most beautiful summer dress I have seen all day. I'm Jason."

She shrinks back in horror. "Is this guy for real?" she thinks. "Does he really think he has a shot with me walking up to me on the street like this?", "Does he know how many Instagram followers do I have?", "Does he know how many men already want me?", "People are really going to think I'm with this guy?", "Disgusting".

She brushes him off like a pest and continues on her way. She arrives her girlfriend's house and they ridicule this guy while taking a new sexy photo to put their Instagram accounts. Life is good for the girls while poor Jason returns home frustrated. They chat together for a time and on her way out of the house, another man approaches her.

He says 'I saw you walking here and I had to come and tell you that you have the most beautiful summer dress I have seen all day. I'm John".

Butterflies instantly flutter into her stomach. Her throat closes up in excitement and anticipation. She gets excited and flattered. She can't stop herself to respond. They chat for 10 minutes and then he tells her he must be going, but that he finds her attractive and he'd like to have coffee with her soon.

She quickly agrees, and says that'd be great. She types her phone number into his phone and they leave each other. She feels so great that she finally found someone she likes; she can't believe this just happened. It feels like destiny.

Sigmund Freud once wrote "The great question that has never been answered, and which I have not yet been able to answer, despite my thirty years of research into the feminine soul, is 'What do women want?'"

Anyone who tell you that they have found an answer on what drives and motivates female attraction and sexual arousal is lying to you. PUAs, dating gurus, female writers, male writers, psychologists, sexologists and biologists have been studying to find it for over a century, and they still couldn't find clear answer.

I go out to approach woman frequently. I approach a beautiful young girl, she looks at me with a serious face, her face falls off, she walks away. I know she hates me and I know that I'm a very unattractive guy for her. At that point I can return back home concluding that I am a unattractive guy and cold approach doesn't work. But I continue. Then, just 30 minutes later, I approach another beautiful young girl. She looks at me, she smiles and starts talking with me. I know she likes me and I know that I'm a very attractive guy for her.

Same day. Same guy. Same beautiful looking young girls. Completely opposite responses. What the fuck?

You may meet with a beautiful girl at any time, any where. But you cannot control the kind of man she likes, her belief about your race, her sexual beliefs coming from her family, her sexual beliefs coming from how society conditioned her, her sexual history with a guy looking like you, her sexual history with a guy approaching her like you, her ovulation cycle, when the last time she had sex was, whether she just had a fight with her boyfriend, whether her dog died, etc.

As men, according to research, we always like a certain characteristics in a woman such as youth, waist ratio, clear skin, shiny hair and smiling face. This is regardless of race, age, culture. The variance in male preference is small. However, with women it can be quite large.

According to a research, while men looked for up to 5 things to get attracted to a woman; women looked up to 250 different things.

Another research has found that women themselves are un-aware of when they're aroused or not. Researchers who tried to draw conclusions by asking women not only come to no conclusions, but they create even more questions about what women want. <u>Women don't even know what they want.</u>

So when you ask a woman how she feels about being ap-proached by a guy on the street, what she really hears is, "How do you feel about being approached by guys like me?"

And the response, of course, is yes, it is an inconvenience and it's creepy because she is not attracted to you. She is not think-ing of the men who approach her whom she wants to approach her. Because their "approaches" do not really fit into the same category.

Put her with him in a room together, and of course they would meet. Doesn't matter in a social circle, subway or in a street, two people who are destined to meet will meet regardless of the setting.

This means every time you cold approach a woman, you meet one of two women. The woman who isn't interested in you and <u>inconvenienced</u> by your approach and the woman who is interested in you and <u>excited</u> by your approach.

According to my research with my past students, friends and my own experiences; if you are an average guy (like me and the rest of us) who will cold approach to 100 girls on the street today; 94 of them on average won't be interested in you, they will be inconvenienced in general and they will turn you down. You will feel kind of frustrated after you approach them.

However, 6 of them on average will think you are attractive and they will be excited of meeting with you. 2 of them will be available to take the interaction to next level such as answering your phone, coming to date or having sex.

So if you stop bitching and complaining about why cold approach doesn't work, why you are not good looking enough, why you are not rich enough or why it's not possible in your country and just go out NOW and approach 100 women, you will most probably have a good time with one of them. I think that's a great return on investment because you can do it in a single day, in a few hours, without spending a dime.

Let's assume that you won't approach 100 today. If you continuously cold approach starting from today for 28 days to 500 women just by spending maximum 1-2 hours a day, I guarantee that you will get rejected many, many times. However, I also guarantee you that you will get great interactions with women, hone your social skills, get dates, get laid or get girlfriends. That's a great return on investment too, if you ask me. Because when you don't cold approach, you are forced to settle for the scraps you're able to get a few times a year at from the social circle or online dating.

Cold Approaching Compared With Social Circle

If you have an average social circle, you may meet one or two attractive women once every 10 outings. However, whenever I go out cold approaching, I meet as many new women as I want.

If I want to meet 10 attractive women in one day, I'll meet 10 attractive women today. Some will be interested; some will not; but I'll have the same results as if I've gone out with my circle 10 times.

If you say that a warm approach is better than cold approach, or where I meet with women has an effect, you are completely wrong.

When you meet with a woman, what is important is your ability to connect with her. This is based on how attractive she finds you and how you present yourself. How you meet or where you meet has absolutely no effect on that.

Think about it logically. If you meet a hot girl on the street, she will still have ten other guys queuing up to meet her in other parts of her life. You still need to stand out, right? If you have met with her in a party of your friend that day, she would still have that 10 guys waiting for her, so you have to stand out.

Remember the girls you slept with or ask a friend who did. If a girl is ever going to sleep with you, she will give you her full attention when you first meet – whether its on the street, in a cafe or in a social circle. I have seen that countless times with tens of girls.

In the social circle, you're dealing with such low quantities of women, you're out of options when she doesn't like you. You will wait for a month to meet with a new hot girl while I can do it in one day.

So, If social circle is your approach, you'll wait... and wait... and wait... and wait... and wait...and of course, you will get lucky and meet a girl someday. She won't be exactly what you want but, well you don't have much options and you need sex. So you will settle into a relationship with her, figuring it'll just be temporary until something better comes along. However nothing better ever will and 10 years later, you're married with kids.

All my friends who thought that cold approach is creepy, met with women through their social circles and married. All of them, <u>without any exception</u>, are bored and tormenting about their wifes now.

All my friends, <u>without any exception</u>, who practiced cold approach either had sex with multiple women they enjoyed before they really found the love of their lives or still continue having sex with multiple women.

The choice is yours.

Cold Approaching Compared With Online Dating

When cold approach compared with online dating, it gets even worse.

According to research, almost 80% of guys who try online dating sites and apps(Tinder!) never go on a single date, despite spending 6 hours a week looking at profiles, then another 7 hours sending out messages. For the rest of the lucky 20%, their dates last only 1.8 hours on average. In fact, some studies have found the average reply rate for women is only 20% in online dating and that number is going down every day.

That means from 100 women, only 5 of them will respond and only 1 will be interested in going to a date with you but if she has the slightest reason to eliminate you, she definitely will because according to that research she will eliminate you 9 out of 10 times. So forget about a relationship or sex, your chances of not being eliminated in the first date is 1000 to 1.

This is why men can't attract the caliber of women they really want to meet and go for the lower quality.

Sexual energy, vibe, eye contact and touch is very important to attraction. Obviously, this is impossible to do through an app. Women are attracted to your sexual energy and confidence. Energy and confidence are very difficult to express with a photo or a description.

Attractive women actually do not benefit directly from online dating anyway. If they are attractive they can meet men anywhere. Guys are flooding their Instagram accounts with messages, why should she spend time in Tinder? It's validation. They get many messages a day that they almost never respond. It's addictive. That's exactly how hot women feel confident about themselves when they meet real men who don't use Tinder.

When that happens, men lower their standards and go for lesser-attractive women. So these women think they are more attractive than they really are and they begin responding to messages more selectively. This continues the inflation cycle.

At the end, guys contact women they'd never speak with in real life and the inflated sexual value of these women make them difficult to meet. The ones you get lucky to meet are the women you'd likely avoid anyways. You know what I'm talking about. Today every "makeup girl" is a fucking Instagram Princess. She looks for the perfect guy but she never asks herself whether she's perfect!

A few years ago, OKCupid surveyed their users on what they found attractive. Not surprisingly, women rated 80% of men are below-average. So if only 20% of men are above average how many of us are good looking?

Obviously these are the standards that we can't meet because most of us are average looking. However, that's not a problem. Since women find sexual energy and confidence attractive, and you can't express that using an app, expressing it in real life is there to save us.

Women dream about being swept off her feet by her prince while sitting in a coffee shop, buying groceries, walking down the street, in a bar or in a party. This is what we all see from the movies. This is what they read in romance novels.

They want to believe that the meeting was a complete chance and something about her was so attractive that the prince felt the need to talk to her. Women want to believe that everything just happened magically. Nothing about online dating is magical. Nothing at all. Nothing. Nothing. Nothing.

The More Spontaneous The Better

To succeed with women you have to meet with real women in real life. Period. The more spontaneous how you meet, the better it is. Period.

Yet a surprising majority of guys rarely leave their houses and they believe they will manifest some pussy from their mobile phone screens or some attractive girl will magically appear in their social circle. They all have one thing in common. <u>They are so fucking afraid to take rejection.</u>

Stating your romantic interest to a woman can embarrassing. That is the necessary part of the process – it is the part where your personal growth will happen. Getting rejected thickens your skin. Each time you get rejected, you become a little bit more comfortable with rejection and a little bit more fine tune yourself.

The more comfortable you are with rejection, the more socially confident you will become. The more confident you become, the more attractive you will be to women. Without exception, anyone who is confident in their abilities has failed many times. Ask any self-made successful person, they will tell you how they failed their way to success.

When you do cold approach, you will sweat and you will bleed. You will push yourself out there, and know that you are being socially awkward, and know that you are being a pest for many women. You will see lots of shit faces. You will see lots of interactions going nowhere. Your ego will take a big hit. You will have days and nights where you feel like a complete social reject, doing something that few other people are doing, looking like an idiot in the process.

I lived that for 14 years and I'm still living it after doing it maybe 10 maybe 15 thousand times and getting many, many results. This is something they can never sell. This is something noone else can teach you. No one can teach you hard work. No one can teach you perseverence. You will teach it to yourself by failing and getting up over and over again. This is the price you pay if you don't want to pay for a Lamborghini to find a gold-digger.

<u>When you cold approach women, you have to see the other side of it.</u>

Because on the other side of it, if you continue doing it and don't let your emotions get in the way, it is a skill set that few men ever possess: <u>the ability to meet with women you like, anytime, anywhere.</u>

When you see a beautiful woman walking down the street, not only you will have a chance to get her, you will also be able to intuit how you should talk with her. That intuition doesn't come from reading or theorizing fucking dating books - it only comes from lots and lots of approaches in lots and lots of different situations, and a mental model informed by many successes and a lot more failures.

Locked away somewhere inside of you is a real you, who is attractive to women, and who is not inconveniencing women when he talks with them. But the only way you will find him is by approaching one woman after another, suffering the social rejection, and refining yourself and your approach a little bit more each time.

Your philosophy must be; <u>go all in with the most raw, sexual, direct and uncensored version of yourself.</u>

Fear, failure, rejection, lust and anger are your friends. Rejection actually increases your confidence but the only way you'll truly understand that rejection increases your confidence is to approach a lot and get rejected. You have to learn the real way – the hard way. <u>There's no way around that.</u>

Rejection Exists For a Reason

Rejection exists to keep people who don't fit each other apart. If a woman rejects you because your are short, or because you are creepy; then you wouldn't going to enjoy being around her anyway. Do you understand the logic here?

Remember your past girlfriends or ask a friend who had one. I remember and I see one thing in common in all of them. Starting from the second we met, she was eager to be with me as I was eager to be with her.

I never ever, ever remember a girl whom I enjoyed who didn't tell me "hell yeah!" when she met with me. I may have fucked some of them but I regret all that time I lost with "maybe" girls because I remember nothing about them and the sex was always mediocre.

Ask yourself: Why would you want to be intimate with someone who doesn't appreciate you? Who are not sure about you? Who say MAYBE or NO to you? Why? Why would you ever settle for such a person? Why would you lose time? Why would you spend money? Why would you care for her? Because she looks beautiful? Because she looks hot? Come on, have some respect for yourself, you deserve better.

Rejection exists to keep people who don't fit each other apart. Rejection must be your tool to eliminate women who won't make you happy. That's the case from the first meeting to a relationship. I say, invite the rejection. It's a means to weed out the women who are not good for you and get to the ones who you will enjoy that much quicker.

This is why we cold approach.

Whether she thinks you a weirdo, or she likes you but you live in different cities, or she's in a horrible mood, whatever the reason; if a woman ever rejects you, it's because she's not compatible with you. Because she doesn't fit to you. If she liked you, she would be willing to work at making it happen. Doesn't matter if you are in the street, bar, club, office, gym or wherever..if she liked you, she would talk. If she wanted you, she would respond.

And if she doesn't, then that just means it's the wrong person or the right person, at the wrong time. And that is fine. <u>Get over it!!!.</u> Use cold approaching as a tool to quickly weed out this type of women and find who really wants you. Because when you take the answer of that bitch as the end result, you really miss that cute girl just around the corner who is dreaming for a person like you. When you finally get that cute girl, you will never remember the bitches who rejected you.

Women are everywhere. Look around, look around, look around. They are like sand in the beach. Go out walking on the streets and look around. Go to a shopping centre and look around. Go to a club and look around. Go to a bar and look around. They are fucking everywhere. If you can't find one, the problem is YOU. <u>Don't bitch and complain, take action.</u>

Increase your chances by going out, especially doing it on the street. Never underestimate the power of street. Never. You don't need to buy vip tables or pay entrance fees in a street. You don't need to deal with jealous girlfriends, bitches, loud playing music, low quality party girls and alcohol.

On the street there is no barrier to beautiful women. They are just walking on the street and when you approach her it's between you and her. This is exactly what you want. While street creates highest approach anxiety to meet with women (since no one does it) there are endless opportunities and adventures you cannot ever imagine.

Don't ever ask yourself if it's weird to approach women on the street or somewhere else. EVERYWHERE is acceptable. EVERYWHERE. Don't think you are inconveniencing them. The fact is, the more spontaneously you meet with her, the better it is. <u>Put yourself out there and do it.</u>

Why You Must Escalate

Once you get over with opening, you will have more advantage than 98% of the man because you will be able to meet with attractive women in a quick succession through cold approaching. However meeting with women doesn't mean you will have sex with them. In order to have sex with women, you must escalate.

Escalation is preparing her for sex by your physical and verbal actions. It includes physical escalation such as touching as well as verbal escalation such as talking sexy. Escalation is critical. If you don't do it, she won't do it for you so you will never get sex from her.

You must escalate because your single goal must be sex before everything else.

Many men will instinctively think that sex isn't everything and really they wish for a "loving relationship" with a woman rather than a quick sex. This is like constructing a building without a foundation.

When you develop a strong sexual relationship with a woman, you have created the platform for the connection that you can enjoy. Trying to get a relationship before the sex will only lead to frustration and it will be the quickest route to being her gay friend.

Where most guys fear is they are afraid of losing the girl if they "push her for sex" such as touching her too soon, touching her too much or being rude by talking sexy.

The fact is; you will never lose a girl by escalating. Never, ever. Ever. Ever. Ever. 1000 times more ever. A girl will forgive a man for pushing too hard but NEVER forgive a man for failing to push hard enough. This is exactly why women ADORE the "bad boy" type guys. Not because they are "bad", but because they have the balls to push hard enough.

If she has any sexual interest in you, you will probably lose her by not escalating. If you approached her and she listens you and responds to you, that's it. She wants to fuck. It's time to escalate. Your goal is to take her your home now and fuck her as if you will never see her again – even if she is going to be your wife.

View escalation as going for what you want. Going for what you want is being a real man. It's very masculine and aggressive. A woman wants to see this within you. If you are attracted to her, go for her. As long as you are respectful and coming from a good place, you have every right to try. Girls do not lead men on if they aren't interested, you have to lead her. So if she's not rejecting you harshly, she's interested.

The golden rule of escalation is "she feels what you feel". When you escalate you really have to get in the moment and get actually turned on yourself. However, you must control your sexual desire. The key to attract her is to purely desire her but not be needy at the same time.

Having strong sexual desire is very attractive. Having an out-of-control sexual desire is unattractive. How do you control that? You use "two steps forward, one step back" rule.

I will explain everything in more detail after week 3 but for example, if you're touching her hand, and she does not remove her hand, it means "it's on". You can now hold her hand when you are walking.

If she doesn't remove your hands when you hold them, then give her a kiss on the cheek then you pull away for a minute or two. Next time when you go for a kiss on the cheek, then progress to the lips.

You need to combine this kind of rapid escalation with coming from a good place, being playful and having respect and love for her, showing her that she is special to you in that moment.

Fear is usually what stops a guy from escalating. When you first touch the hands of the girl, don't think that it's awkward. Look at her and smile, show her that you are doing it because you want to do it in the moment. Tell her that you really wanted to know how it feels to touch her without a single shame.

Even if you are the most awkward guy she has seen, It's better to try and come across as a pervert than to do nothing and play it safe. When you play it safe you will be just another guy from Tinder. You will be mediocre.

Seduction is a competition, especially in big cities. Being mediocre can't be your option. Every guy wants his part of the cake. Are you going to let them get in your way? Are you going to let them take what you want? You will only have one chance with a hot girl because she has so many choices.

What makes the difference is whether you make her wet or not in her extremely short attention span. That's why you have to be aggressive. You have to look meeting and seducing her as a hunt and you have to see her as a prey who can run away in a moment.

You Are Not Making Friends

You are not meeting with women to make friends. You are doing it to seduce her and fuck her. Don't let any let's-be-friends bullshit creep into you.

You are a predator hunting prey. You are approaching women and giving them a strong sexual invitation from the beginning. You are a sexual threat for her. And this is ok because you are on a hunt where the prey want to be taken. Many of them already horny and you make the rest horny by your sexual invitation. All women want and like sex more than you.

You don't get the girl when she finds out that you have common hobbies. You don't get the girl when she finds out that you are a doctor. You get the girl when you are standing in front of the girl talking about bullshit while electricity crackles between you. Your eyes are locked, you caress her hand and you both know exactly how dirty it is and you both know exactly that you are going to fuck each other. This is how you get the girl.

Always escalate. Think of a child who wants a toy. He doesn't need the toy but he wants it so much that he wants to grab it and he wants to play with it. Make your sexual intent completely clear while letting her know that you are a non-needy and patient hunter who may not eat until he gets what he wants to eat.

In this way you will not be manipulated by her shit tests, ploys, acts and trips. You will be different than all those so called PUAs and dating gurus. When you are authentic and non-needy about your desire, you take away her power to play with you. You are making your no bullshit unashamed sexual offer: "take it now or leave it".

Look deep into her eyes and project thoughts. Look at her, imagine fucking her in every position, and feel your erection. What thoughts and desires appear in your head when you're looking at her face, imagining these things? Tell her that playfully without any single shame.

Touch her as she is already your lover. Make her feel your energy. Feel your erection and touch her, as if you are transferring your sexual energy from your dick to her.

Think of how you speak with your girlfriend before you have sex. Your voice is slow, your eyes are like a tiger stalking the prey, you touch her as you want. You know that you will fuck her soon and you are just in the moment. This is the state you have to be in.

Constantly pushing yourself to convey sexual intent makes it progressively easier to do so because you are making your sexuality a habit. You get used to seeing girls as sexual beings, as sexual objects. Objectify women. She may logically tell you that's its rude, but you will soon begin to see that doing that is the greatest compliment you can give to a woman. She'll love you for it.

This is exactly how real love is created. This is exactly how you get a great relationship. This is exactly how you get hot passionate sex. They are not created by telling DHV stories, they are not created by trying to be confident, they are not created by being rich or good looking, they are not created by your mutual interests. They are created by pure non-needy raw sexual desire. Read any romance novel and you will understand what I mean.

Listen to your instincts

Quiet, dark, alone. Alone in your head, alone with that buzz no one but you can feel. No outside comments. No distraction. No Fear. No Anxiety. No Doubt. Right now, it's all about you. You are enough. You can do it. Your desire pushes you, burns in you, drives you. You do it. You are totally in the moment. You can hear your heart, you control every beat. You control everything. "In your own little world," you are. You're in the zone.

When you go out to meet with women, your aim has to get into the zone. Because once you step into the zone, you are detached from everything on the outside. What is everything on the outside? It's the bullshit you used to think and they used to say. It's everything you can generate with "I'm not X enough".

When you are in the zone, nothing can affect you. No fear, no distraction, no intrusion. Total concentration. You're not thinking, because thinking turns your thoughts on to everything except the task at hand, and the zone is about the opposite, turning your thoughts off to everything except the task at hand.

Thinking takes you away; the zone keeps you where you need to be. That's your safe haven: no headaches, no limiting beliefs. The headaches and limiting beliefs will still be there when you're done, but until you're done, you have to get to that place where you control time and space. You have to get into zone.

Picture a lion running wild. He stalks his prey, attacking and killing, and then goes in search of his next conquest. That's what his lion instincts tell him to do, he doesn't know anything else. He's not misbehaving, he's not bad, he's being a lion.

Now lock him up in the zoo. He lies there all day, quiet and lethargic and well fed. What happened to those powerful instincts? They're still there, deep inside, waiting to be uncaged. Let him out of the zoo and he goes lion again, preying and attacking. Put him back in the cage, he lies down.

Most people are the lion in the cage. Safe, tame, waiting for something to happen. However, for humans, the cage isn't made of steel bars; it's made of bad advice, low self-esteem, bullshit rules and tortured thinking about what you can't do or what you're supposed to do.

It's molded around you by a lifetime of overthinking and overanalyzing and worrying about what could go wrong. Stay in the cage long enough, you forget those basic instincts. But they're there, right now, waiting for you to find the key to the cage so you can finally stop thinking about what you'll do if you ever get out. All that killer instinct is just waiting to attack.

Ask yourself. What's stopping you? Have you ever talked with a woman you were attracted to and everything went well? If you say no, I'll ask again. Can you talk with a woman you are attracted to?

Of course you can.

Then why are you still questioning your ability to do it by reading this book? Why are you not out there meeting and talking with women right now? Because at some point, you stopped trusting yourself.

Everything You Need Is Already Inside You
Let me tell you one thing and this is the most important advice you can get from me.

Everything you need is already inside you. You are completely wired with instincts and reflexes specifically designed so you can survive, reproduce and succeed. You don't have to think about using them, they're always working. You just have to go out there and do it.

That's how I want you to envision your instincts. No thinking. Just the gut reaction that comes from being so sure about yourself, that there's nothing to think about.

If you're riding a bike, and suddenly the car ahead of you slams on its brakes, do you pause to consider all your options or stop to ask for advice? No, you slam on the brakes. No thought, no hesitation. Instant response, based on instinct.

When you see a woman you are attracted to, you don't need to think and analyze the situation to decide talking with her. You just make the decision. Your instincts become so finely tuned that you have a reflexive response that allows you to "just do it" without thinking. In other words, you're in the zone.

Meeting and seducing women is not a science. It's an instinct. Instinct is the opposite of science: research tells you what others have learned, instinct tells you what you have learned.

Believe what you know about yourself. You already know what to do. The women you want are out there on the street, in a cafe, at work, in the gym. They are everywhere. Stop what you heard and go with your instincts. Stop waiting to be taught something you already know.

Do you think all those babies are done by doing "game"? Do you think all those men who have beautiful women in their lives read books, took courses and listened to fucking dating advice? Do you think all those men are rich? Do you think they are all good looking?

No! They just went there and did it. You are reading this book already knowing what you have to do. You are just waiting for someone to tell you. Instead of just going out there doing it and learning by yourself, you sat down with a book to analyze the situation. Trust me: no one ever slept with someone new sitting on the couch.

That's why I won't be teaching you anything about the techniques and specifics of meeting and seducing women before the third week because you actually don't really need them. In these two weeks we will only focus on taking action, foundations and your mindset.

Here is how you must meet and seduce women for the rest of your life. A few words are enough because really, everything you need is already inside you and most probably you have used them before.

When you see a woman you really like, clear your mind of everything and focus on her. Focus on her beauty. Look at her ass. Imagine that ass in front of you and your cock sliding in and out of her pussy. Look at her breasts. Imagine sucking on them while she is riding you.

First, feel the desire running through your body, and then approach her. Your desire has to override your approach anxiety.

Tell her that you saw her walking past and you liked how she looked, so you came to say hi to her. Then tell her what you liked about her and build upon it in a playful conversation.

It doesn't have to be perfect. If your energy is right, anything you say will sound perfect. If you are coming from an authentic place and you have a raw desire her, just saying "hi" is actually enough. If your energies match, she will stay, regardless of what you say and everything will be fine.

She may reject you or she may respond to you. Accept the result. Accept yourself if she rejects. Accept that it's ok. If she responds, talk with her as if you are going to fuck her today, because you will. Believe in it. Give your masculine energy and excitement to her.

When she is talking, look deeply in her eyes, then look at her breasts and imagine coming on to them in a few hours. Imagine her lips sucking your cock. I want you to get an erection when you are talking with her. I want you to imagine the raw sex with her. I want you to be an animal. Yes, I want you to be a pervert – but coming from a good place.

I want you to give yourself permission to feel this way because you are letting your natural instincts to take over. They will override any fear and boring conversation. Forget about what to say and let your natural instincts do the work. Before the approach, after the approach and until you get sex; there is no force more powerful than your natural instincts. Your raw sexual energy is your most powerful force that you must use.

You've grown up in a society where all of the savagery of nature taken out out of life. Modern society is purposefully designed to separate you from your masculine essence. At school you are punished and drugged for showing signs of aggression and independence. At work you are slaved for obedience.

You have to go back to your masculine core. This is the engine for all action, your basic raw material of manliness. Most modern men have a brain loaded with society conditioning including the "game" and dating advice which cripple all of their thinking. Fear and anxiety come from that exact place of being "not enough", "game" and "dating". <u>You have to un-fuck all that.</u>

You need to revert back to being a caveman. Cavemen think "woman, want fuck" and goes to get the girl. Caveman doesn't talk, his masculine energy gets the girl.

This is what you need to be doing. This creates the attraction. This creates the love. This is how you get and stay in the zone. This is being present and when you are present, you will have access to powers of creativity and energy that you probably didn't know you have.

Assignments

Assignment 1

You will approach 10 women today. You will do it no matter what. You have 3 choices to do it. These are the "unconventional ways" to demolish approach anxiety I was talking about because very few use them. People use willpower that never works until you get used to doing it.

1-using your sexual energy.

2-with your friend, using him to push you.

3-using bethabit.com with the incentive of losing money if you don't approach.

Choose one of them at the start but you should choose the the first one in the long run.

If you have been going out to approach women to come home without saying hi to even one of them, it will be hard to do it today. If you have never done it, it may not be easy. If you have any doubts, I strongly recommend you to get the help of a friend or create a challenge in Bethabit. This is a 28 day program and if you can't approach 10 women today, you won't do it tomorrow and most probably you will quit. So guarantee yourself at the start that you will do it no matter what.

Good way to guarantee is to call your friend and ask him to meet with you. Go to a crowded place one hour before your meeting and try to do it yourself using your sexual energy. If you can't do it, make your friend help you do it. As I said you can create a Bethabit challenge the day before to give yourself no chance as well.

I repeat. This is not a bullshit theory book, this is all about action and you will approach 10 women today, 500 women in 28 days in total. This is the very key of getting successful with women. It's just like sales. If you don't advertise your product, you won't get leads, and you won't sell. Even you have the worst product, by advertising, you can get more leads and eventually make more sales to get the feedback and belief to improve your product. If you meet with women daily, you will always have abundance of women regardless of your circumstances. So choose one of the ways below, burn the bridges and you will be proud of yourself at the end of 28 days. If you won't do it, stop reading this book. Stop and continue reading after you do day 1 assignments. I will write more about how you can take action below:

Using Your Sexual Energy
The most effective way to overcome approach anxiety or the fear of meeting women is using your sexual energy. If you let any logical thinking guide you, chances are you won't be able to do it consistently until you really get used to doing it everyday. Because once you let your logic run you, your brain will always find a reason not to approach. Your "bitch" brain will always take the less risky way because it will want to protect your ego. However, if you let your sexual energy run you, you reptilian brain will override your neocortex and not only you will make the approach, you will make her reptilian brain override her neocortex.

Making her reptilian brain override her neocortex is the key here. Know that, even an average girl always has at least 10 men she can "logically" choose from Tinder, Instagram, her work, social circle, etc. If you let her logic run her mind, she will most probably choose a more logical choice than you. However, if you let her sexuality override her logic, then she will act according to her sexuality to choose you. How do you do that? You become sexual yourself first, then you transfer your sexual energy to her by going up to her by direct sexual intent.

You may use the help of your friend or Bethabit if you are uncomfortable meeting with women at the start. However, ultimately, you must go out alone being hungry for sex and meet with women solely using that sexual energy. That will give you the real results you want.

Using the help of a friend

Do the same thing you would do alone by the help of a friend. Ask him to spend an hour with you to push you every 300 seconds. Give him $100 to lose if you don't approach every 300 seconds. Help him to do the same thing for himself. Tell him "man, me and you are going to fucking do this together...and you are going to me on my ass if I start slacking and I'm going to be on your ass if you start slacking..and we'll never accept mediocre again!!!" If he doesn't answer you "Hell yeah, let's do it!!"..leave him and find someone who will. You can very well use "wingman" forums to find like minded people. Walk together with your friend and approach every 300 seconds with turns. After an hour you will be able to do it alone. Leave each other and start doing it alone. You must get used to doing it alone. If you can't find a friend at all or your friend doesn't come regularly, then hire an university student 1-2 hour every weekday to help you. Don't ever pay for a coach. Invest that little amount until you get used to doing it alone. Risk your $100 again, let him count 300 seconds for you and do your daily approaches no matter what. Don't be ashamed for anything, be ashamed for not taking action and get used to doing it alone as soon as possible.

Using Bethabit

Bethabit is my challenge site you can use to challenge yourself in 41 different areas. Approaching women daily is one of them. The site works by you depositing money and risking it to lose if you don't approach daily, just like you did with your friend by giving him $100. You will record your approaches using your phone using Bethabit app or any other camera/app and send links to us for approval. It's guaranteed way to make you approach every single day for 28 days. It worked perfectly well with my other clients. I strongly recommend you to use it.

Assignment 2

Write your daily journal that answers these questions. This is a must. Without doing this you will never see your improvement and you will never remember how you succeeded when the hard times come. Write as openly as possible.

- What happened today, Which girls you talked, how did they respond?
- How do you feel yourself?
- What did you learn today?
- What will you do differently tomorrow?

DAY 2 - GET INTO THE ZONE | OVERCOME APPROACH ANXIETY

Be Aware of Your Ego

Approach anxiety comes from lack of self-acceptance resulting from low self-esteem. It doesn't come from evolutionary fear of getting killed by the tribe's leader or any of that bullshit. Your ego creates a delusional reality that you are high value. When you do something that risks losing your value, your ego protects you.

Say you're walking down the street, and a beautiful girl comes towards you. She is sexy as hell, exactly your type. What do you do?

If you are inexperienced, then you will probably do nothing because you will most likely be afraid to approach her because if she rejects you, you'll be crushed. If you are an experienced, you still may not do anything. Why? because this time you're afraid that if you approach her and she rejects you, your status as the "guy who is great with women" will be compromised.

In both of the cases the real reason for not approaching is protection of your ego. After all, it's far easier to make excuses and do nothing rather than putting yourself on the line and risk failure. However, this is a sabotage for yourself because <u>the more women you approach, the more likely you'll end up having sex.</u>

Think of sales. Succeeding in finding a woman you like is no different than succeeding in sales (getting rich). Say you have a shitty product. When you expose that to 1000 people, 1 will buy. Say you have a ordinary product. When you expose that to 1000 people, 10 will buy. Say you have a great product. When you expose it to 1000, 50 will buy. At the end of the day, by advertising, you can sell any product.

There are things you can do to improve how attractive you are, such as mainly your sexual energy, how you look, the quality of your opening and your escalation but in the end it's entirely a numbers game. It's a numbers game of matching energies. If your energies match you'll be on the way to get her. You project her your sexual energy, but she has to be receptive for that. Finding that receptive girl means doing the numbers game by approaching over and over again.

So there are no shortcuts. That's why the truly successful seducer never says that he is enough and he approaches all the time. To make progress in meeting women, actually anything in life, you must engage directly with reality. You must welcome raw unfiltered feedback. That's how you will improve yourself. That's how people make a shitty product a great product.

I know that it's not easy to just go out there and put yourself on the line over and over again. I know it's emotionally draining. Walking around the streets, watching pretty young girls pass by and then trying to work up the motivation to approach them and risk rejection.

It's hard work and it's painful. However, you have to accept the reality. You will be approaching different types of women and they will give different responses. Do not let their feedback challenge your core self-worth. Do not let negative experiences settle into your identity and exaggerate the positive experiences. It's not only you doing that. I've done that, remember me. Go watch the guys on youtube, they've done that. Remember them. Remember that you are not alone and you are doing the right thing.

Do whatever it takes, but do not quit. You can read 1000 motivational books, watch 1000 motivational Youtube videos. Let me tell you what they say. they say, do not quit. What you want can really be just around the corner.

When you walk up to a girl and hit on her, it shouldn't matter how she reacts. She laughs and two days later you fuck her? Great! She brushes you off right away? No big deal. Get used to it by doing it over and over again. That will create the "thick skin" you need. Next one. Next one. Next one. Go on!

Neither the highs nor the lows can change that identity that is you. Don't lose sight of the big target. You are trying to find someone who will make you happy. So as long as you are going out and trying, you are on the right track.

Operate On Your Own Truth

Most men, when they approach women they like, they think like, "I hope she won't reject me.". It's about her. How about thinking, "I wonder if she's my girl?". Think about yourself, not her. Because it's not about you.

There are millions of circumstances completely outside of your control and at any given time, the women you will meet and talk are going to be experiencing one of them. The best you can do is to let it go and remember: it's not about you.

Put yourself in her shoes. Maybe she had a bad day in her job. Maybe her cat just died and she didn't feel like talking. Maybe her ex-boyfriend has been calling her and harassing her and she just wants to be left alone. Maybe the last guy who came up and talked to her grabbed her ass so she's upset. Maybe the guy she went out with last night was totally rude and looked just like you. Maybe she just didn't like how you look. Think about yourself. It's not about you, it's about her.

As Tyler Durden says in Fight Club; "Stop trying to control everything and just let go!" See every rejection simply as an incompatibility. Whether she thinks you are a weirdo, or whether she is crazy about you but she has a boyfriend, if a woman ever rejects you, it's because she's not compatible with you for some reason.

Find Your Perfect Girl

You've probably noticed that some girls turn your head and your friends don't like them. Conversely, your friend may like a girl and you may think she is average. Generally speaking, our DNA causes us to be attracted to women whose DNA will offer us things we don't have. It comes from the "opposites attract" law.

When I see my perfect girl it's like my blood is bubbling. She pulls me. I feel an uncontrollable motion towards her. I know in my gut that I can get her and she will want me. I somehow feel it. It's an instinct of me. Such a girl will attract you so strongly that approach anxiety is significantly reduced.

I use the fantasy of finding my perfect girl as a motivation to go further. This way, I don't attach much importance to other girls I meet. I see a beautiful brunette in a business suit coming down the street. I know she is not my type. I know these kind of girls do not respond to me.

However, I still approach her just because she is hot and I can never know what will come out. I don't get excited though. I just give her shot. I don't attach much importance to her. I know what I really want. I actually use her as an exercise. I chat with her to lift my mood. Because of doing this, when I finally find my perfect girl, I am usually in a great vibe.

How do you find your perfect girl? Know the qualities you like in a woman. Be specific.

For example; I like slavic women with colored hair, casual clothes and nerdy characteristics. I don't like business women, I don't like party girls, I don't like posh girls, I don't like brands and expensive purses. I like those cute programmers and graphic designers. No-one is more sexy for me than a medium height redhead with nerdy glasses and a summer dress.

Everyone dresses and acts publicly in ways consistent with their self-image because humans are always signaling who they are and the identity choices they have made. I can spot the girls I like very easily. Define the exact characteristics of the girl you like. Then imagine finding a girl like her and fucking her. Finding her must compel you to go out, make approaches, be social and get ready to meet with her.

When you finally find your perfect girl, everything will compel you to talk with her. No fear. No doubt. Total confidence that comes from the rejections you took that day. You won't be thinking. You will begin the interaction with her from a position of deeply felt masculine interest. Raw sexual desire.

This is genuine. You are in a position where you can be completely honest with her and it will enhance your chances of making a connection. These will be the girls who get deeply attracted to you.

Use Intervals

I was losing too much time searching for my perfect girl.

I could easily approach the girls I like and get results but I realized that at the end of the day I was walking 3-4 hours to approach 8 to 15 girls and actually meet with 1 or 2 of them. That was a loss of time and energy. I had more important things to do.

Then I realized a clear pattern. It was always hard to start a day, but when I started approaching, I could do it again soon. However, if I've quit approaching for some reason such a harsh rejection, I would stop for a long time such as an hour. Then I would gather my confidence to start again and do the same process until the next "crash". I was either stopping after taking the rejection personal and getting angry, or I was stopping after getting a number that I knew would result with a date.

So next time I got out I started to be aware of this pattern and I started to control that by giving 5 minutes between each approach. Then, everything changed. My daily approach count increased by three times while time I spent decreased 2 times. That lead me to use intervals consistently.

Train Everyday

You have to see the session of meeting with women like a training session in the gym because it's actually training your social muscles, sexual energy and confidence.

Seeing meeting with women as training will make you lose approach anxiety because you will always "stay in shape". So as long as you stay "stay in shape", not only you have constant flow of new girls coming to you daily, but you will also integrate meeting women with your daily life.

The more you repeat the same actions, the more they will become a part of you. So when you see your perfect girl in a business meeting you attend or a in a bus, you won't miss her.

This is the program I do and recommend you to follow it. It consists of "warm up", "action" and "free flow" phases.

Warm Up Session

At 17:30 I go to a very crowded place where people go out of work.

I go to middle of that place, stand there and say to myself that "I can fuck up as much as I can until 18:00 because I am only interested in nerdy looking slavic blonde girls who finish working after 18:00". I take all the pressure out of myself first by putting my focus on finding my perfect girl.

I say to myself "everybody will look at me and I will look stupid and its ok because this is the price I have to pay by not choosing to settle being a provider guy". I say myself quotes from fight club such as "It's only after we've lost everything that we're free to do anything". I intentionally destroy my ego and try to enjoy from that by smiling, faking it even I can't.

Then I start by approaching any girl who is 6 or better out of 10. The interval is always 300 seconds. I must choose one until 300. After I talk with her another 300 starts.

I must always be direct. I get aroused as much as I can. I must go and tell that she looks nice - simple as that. I don't care if I talked right, stopped her right, etc. I am there to fuck up. Everybody has to look at me and everybody has to see and realize what I'm doing. I want them to see me, I want the girls to reject me and I want to teach my brain that everything is ok. All I want is to connect with my sexuality and teach my brain that "it's ok, there is nothing to worry". I approach a girl and come back to my place. Then approach more girls and come back to my place. This goes on for 30 minutes.

Action Session

At 18:00 I start walking around the same crowded place. After 18:00 people go out of work so places get crowded with nice looking girls. This time I know that I have to find my perfect girl and I know that while I walk around I won't be recognized as I did when I was warming up. I accept that I won't expect anything else from my other approaches. I remind myself that I know what I want. I continue to approach any woman who is 6 or better with 300 second intervals because I know that I have to be "in shape" when I finally see my perfect girl. Again, I try to get aroused by women as much as I can.

As long as I keep the momentum, approach anxiety almost disappears at the end of this hour. I approach anyone I would fuck without putting myself pressure on the outcome.

Freeflow Session

At 19:00, I leave that crowded place and start walking on the streets of the city. I see myself like a shark looking for prey. I walk slowly and surely patrolling the streets. I get into the zone. I'm fully sexual at this time. I still keep 300 second intervals because at 19:00 city becomes full of people and that gives me the possibility. I walk until 20:00 to come back home. Best results come usually in this 1 hour because of my fully warmed-up state.

Sometimes nothing comes out, but when it comes out, %80 percent of the time I find my perfect girl in this time frame. When I see her, I approach her with full sexual intent. If I ever get results, I get results from these girls and eventually these make me happy. The reason is because I don't give a seducer or pickup artist vibe to her. I give a natural vibe. She really thinks that I am a guy just saw her on the street, dazzled and came up to her with genuine desire, not being able to stop his attraction to her.

However, if I haven't crushed my ego in the first hour by getting that much rejections and kept the momentum by still approaching to get even more rejections, I would never approach her with full sexual intent and come up like a natural. The key is not losing the momentum. As momentum builds, less and less effort is needed and it becomes more and more effortless as you become more and more fearless. Your skin gets thicker and you finally hit the jackpot.

It's daily. When I get up the next day, I will be the guy with approach anxiety again and I will have to go through the same process again. Every single day I start as a shy person and build my confidence up. Confidence is something you build up daily.

Use intervals as I do. Use my workout program. I use this three step process to spend my 2-3 hour most effectively to reach success. If you don't have any woman in your life, go out everyday for 2-3 hours until you find sex. If you find sex but not consistently or not with a girlfriend you like/love, then go out 5 days a week for 1-2 hours. If you find a girlfriend you like/love then still go out 3 times a week for 1-2 hours. See it as going to the gym. If you do this, you will always have an abundance of good women in your life.

Assignments

Approach 10 Women
Approach 10 women as I have written on day 1.

Write Your Daily Journal
Write your daily journal as I have written on day 1.

DAY 3 - CREATE RAW SEXUAL DESIRE | THINK LIKE A CAVEMAN

Genuinely Desire Her

I repeat. <u>The best way you can attract, seduce and sleep with a woman is to desire her genuinely.</u>

Do you believe that men and women -really- get together because they feel desire and passion for each other or is it about finances, common interests, hobbies and friendship?

You have to identify this desire right in your cock and balls. Your dick has to get rock hard when you look at her. When you meet with her and when you are talking with her; only thing you can think of should be how it would be like to fuck her hard today. Nothing else. No intellectualisation. No relationship stuff. Nothing else but pure animalistic desire.

Your desire has to be like a child sees a toy and wants it, grabs it. The child feels no other conflicting emotions about it, doesn't worry about what she is thinking. It just wants that toy! You have to be the same about a woman without any shame. Desiring a woman like this is the best compliment you can give to her. It's extremely refreshing for her. You have to use that desire to push you to action. It is more overpowering than any negative emotion such as fear of rejection.

Getting laid is not hard or complicated once a man becomes in tune with his masculinity and his masculine desires. Desire is a key component of any seduction you may run on her. You cannot logically persuade a woman to like you. "Attraction is not a choice".

If you want her to like you, you can display characteristics such as having high self-esteem, non-neediness, being centered, having integrity and sticking to your own standards. But if you want to fuck her, then all you need to do is to purely desire her.

I repeat, getting laid is not hard or complicated if you are in tune with your desire. When you meet her, you don't have to be smooth. It may not always look pretty. It can be boring and lacking in fun. It doesn't even have to involve being social. You don't even have to like each other.

I've fucked girls who didn't like me. Logically, socially, financially we were not fit for each other. She didn't like how I looked at all. She didn't like anything about my world view. We had nothing in common. But I fucked her because I used my sexual energy. The beauty of the girl, her scent, the way she moves, the feeling of her pussy on my cock and balls. I was in the moment. When I looked at her, I drank her in. So she slept with me, <u>even though she didn't intend to do it at all.</u>

When you really desire a woman without any conflicting emotions, you don't have to talk much. Don't think it's your words that are getting the girl. You are speaking to her in the hard-coded physical language of the caveman, the language that got caveman laid before spoken language evolved. The words are just the things that fill the space while you lay your raw sexual desire in her.

Unfortunately, in modern society, men have been domesticated. We still have teeth, but we also wear a muzzle. We've been trained to misidentify with our raw sexuality. We've learned to be polite, nice, agreeable to keep our "status" very "well". This is just as much a disaster for women as it is for men, because only men who are in tune with their primal sexual nature can make them feel how they want to feel.

If you can learn to take off the muzzle that other men are wearing, you will be dangerous, but you will also be exciting. This part of you is raw, it's focused, it's simple. It does not need to prove itself, it doesn't care what others think, it is pure, unadulterated desire. It's definitely not what society wants from you.

Learn to tap into this part of you and your results will sky-rocket. The biggest aphrodisiac in the world is someone who likes you, genuinely likes you. A woman's desire is to be desired. But it has to be genuine and raw desire.

It can't be a, "I'll desire you as long as you boost my ego and impress my co-workers", a kind of desire. Beautiful women have been conditioned for most of their lives to know when a man is being genuine or not, whether the compliment is a gift or a bartering tool.

Get in tune with your raw desire for women, and you will be naturally motivated to take the actions you need to take to get what you want. That primal raw desire is powerful, and it's your raw desire for a woman that will overwhelm her and make her lose control of herself.

Attraction is not a choice. As German philosopher Arthur Schopenhauer pointed out, one can choose what to do, but not what to want.

The Modern Caveman

I come from a very dysfunctional family and a school life. Getting beat, bullied, ridiculed and being fat wasn't easy. Thank god, I could manage to lose weight by university using intermittent fasting(going to write book about that!). I guess because of fasting, when I was in university, I was a horny guy. I had very little 'game' and self confidence but I was horny. After all those years of being alone and masturbating, I wanted to have sex, finally. I used to go to clubs with my nerd friends. When I went out, my underlying motivation wasn't self-development, and it wasn't to make friends. It was much less complicated than that. I was just horny and I wanted to have sex so fucking badly.

My goal was to meet a girl and fuck her ASAP. My friends were doing the "game" stuff of Ross Jeffries. I thought it was too complicated. They knew all the material, had done thousands of approaches, and thought about the speed seduction stuff all the time. Somehow, I didn't.

What I observed was; they wanted to get laid as much as I did but their actions didn't reflect their real desires. I was just horny and even though I wasn't confident at all, my actions clearly reflected my desires. Even though I was afraid, I would go up to her like an animal and try to talk with her. Because I was really horny and didn't think anything else other than sex, the girls were responding.

But when my friends were out, they had a number of agendas competing with each other. Sure, getting laid was one, but it wasn't their predominant motivation. They wanted to look cool in front of their friends, they wanted to overcome "AA", they wanted to overcome their insecurities, they wanted to avoid offending women, they wanted to practice their game, etc.

I finally fucked a girl. The first thing I said when I saw her was "Damn. I want to fuck her".

As men, we all have a raw, primal, uncomplicated sexual side that sees an attractive woman and thinks nothing more than, "Damn. I want to fuck her". We all have a caveman inside. All we need is to let that caveman run us.

We Are Biologically Polygamous

If asked to imagine what prehistoric human sex was like, according to psychologist Christopher Ryan, most of us would image "the caveman, dragging a woman by her hair with one hand, a club in the other hand". Ryan says this image is mistaken in every detail in his book Sex at Dawn. A much more likely picture of how it went down in prehistoric times was "a caveman would quietly sit in the corner and watch another caveman have sex with a woman, patiently waiting his turn". Just like what American Indians did.

Ryan argues that while chimpanzees are our close relatives, our closest relatives are in fact bonobos. Bonobos live in female-centered societies, where war is rare and sex serves an important social function. They are polygamous, with both male and female apes having regular sex with multiple partners.

According to his research, Ryan concludes that no group-living nonhuman primate is monogamous, and extreme adultery and polygamous relationships has been documented in every human culture. He says, sex for pleasure with various partners is therefore more "human" than animal. Strictly reproductive, once-in-a-blue-moon sex is more "animal" than human. In other words, an excessively horny monkey is acting "human," while a man or woman uninterested in sex, strictly speaking, "acting like an animal".

Why is monogamy so difficult today even society pushes it? Why do more than half of the marriages end up with divorce? Because we are biologically programmed against it. In fact, the human organism is designed for the exact opposite of that. We are, both men and women are designed to me polygamous.

However, if human were polygamous, capitalism would never work.

It was not until the advent of agriculture that man developed a notion of private property, and had reason to feel jealous of a promiscuous mate. Culture invented monogamy, and with it marriage, cheating, and a sense of shame that surrounds our sexual selves.

These behaviors are not biologically programmed traits of our species. When viewed against the full scale of our species' existence, ten thousand years after agriculture is a very brief moment. Even if we ignore the roughly two million years since the emergence of Homo Sapiens, anatomically modern humans are estimated to have existed as long as 200,000 years.

The amount of time our species has spent living in settled agricultural societies represents just 5 percent of our collective experience, at most. For the 95% of our times in this world, we were living like a caveman and having sex all the time with different partners of the tribe.

That's why I say, <u>we should go back to our nature if we want to naturally attract woman.</u> It's in our genes.

Convey Your Sexual Desire

So how do you go back to your nature? So how do you get so sexually hungry as the caveman? How do you get lots of sex as caveman did? How do you find the caveman in you?

I will come to quitting masturbation and eating right in more detail in the coming days but before that, most importantly, everything starts in your head.

You have to strip away all the bullshit you've accumulated over the past years and reconnect with what was always inside you: that raw masculine essence that is running through your veins right now. This is a mindset. In order to take out that mindset you have to continuously visualize being sexual. That's the main solution.

Constantly pushing yourself to convey sexual intent makes it progressively easier to do so because you are forming a new habit at a higher default level of sexuality. You take away the power of rejection. You get used to seeing women as sexual creatures. "Sexual objects" I should say. They love that even though they would may logically tell they don't.

A lot of men don't give themselves permission to feel this way. Their natural desire is mixed with other conflicting emotions such as the fear that she will reject him, he is not rich enough, if he is not good looking enough, if he is not young enough, etc. In other words it is mixed up with other feelings which kills the pure, animal state.

There is no force more powerful than your natural instincts and they are more important for her than your money or looks. Cavemen thinks "girl, want fuck". This is how you need to be thinking. It has to make you want to talk to her and give it your best shot with nothing else on your mind. This in other words means being present, in other words, being in the zone. She feels that instantly.

A woman has to know you want her in a deep level. Showing your masculine desire for a woman unapologetically is going to turn her on like nothing else. Showing that desire through your eyes will have her hypnotized by you. With desire you will get laid a lot. It's as simple as that and this should be what you want. If she comes to you because of your car, be sure that she will go to somebody else with a better car. This is how you make her fall in love with you. Just you.

Give a guy the very basics of talking with women, send him out and with enough desire he will start getting laid. Women are easy to men who show them sexual desire unapologetically and in a manly direct way. Don't hide, push down, or divert your desires. Don't waste it on porn and don't let it never built up by having a horrible diet. When the desire is there, the way will appear.

If you're not getting laid then check your desire but nothing else. Use it as energy to fuel you and create sparks between you and the women you are going to meet. That is what it is there for, that is what it was created for, so use it as caveman used it.

Assignments

Approach 10 Women

Approach 10 women as I have written on day 1.

Write Your Daily Journal

Write your daily journal as I have written on day 1.

DAY 4 - CREATE RAW SEXUAL DESIRE | LIVE CAVEMAN LIFESTYLE

Importance of High Testosterone

Scientists believe that testosterone is the key component to male sex drive and it does play a vital role in male sexual desire. Problem is, our modern lifestyle is testosterone's worst enemy. In the last 100 years men's testosterone levels declined 4 times and the trend is continuing to decline every year. Think about how much testosterone caveman had!

Lack of testosterone includes low sex drive, difficulty achieving an erection, low semen volume, hair loss, loss of muscle, lack of motivation, personality changes, and anxiety. It can also present as self-destructive behaviors like gambling, alcoholism and smoking. Testosterone deficiency even leads to higher rates of cardiovascular disease, type 2 diabetes, and bone fractures.

There are mainly two problems with modern lifestyle. First; we are physically and mentally inactive. Second, everyday, crap is being pumped into our bodies.

Our diets are embarrassing. Instead of eating like our ancestors and like the hunters that we all are, we eat a diet fit for a barnyard animal. Our culture sees meat and fat as the enemy, while carbs and sugars are treated like gold.

High fructose corn syrup is in almost everything you buy, and sugar is known to wreak absolute havoc on our endocrine systems. Food companies are well aware that all this stuff is destroying you, but as long as people continue to buy they will continue to produce it.

We are also incredibly nutrient deficient. In order to function properly and create the testosterone that we need to, we need certain vitamins and minerals. The most important being vitamin A, vitamin C, vitamin D, magnesium and zinc. Vitamin D alone is a ridiculous deficiency that plagues almost 85% of people in the world. And forget about Zinc & magnesium, most people don't even touch that.

You must increase your testosterone levels because testosterone is directly related with the raw sexual desire I am talking about.

In order to increase your testosterone levels, first you will need to say no to most commercial modern foods. You can have a huge increase in testosterone levels by just changing your diet alone. What I will tell are all backed up with research and they only relate to testosterone. These are the main rules to increase your testosterone.

Rules to Increase Testosterone

Up Your Cholesterol

You have to eat whole eggs, avocado, nuts, olive oil, coconut oil, butter, shrimp and similar healthy oily foods. When it comes to boosting testosterone, cholesterol is your best friend. Testosterone is literally made from cholesterol and without it you would have none. It has been proven that there is no relation between cholesterol intake and heart attack as doctors once thought. The real enemy is actually sugar and grains.

Eat Vegetables

Broccoli and other veggies actually reduce estrogen levels in your body, thus promoting higher testosterone levels. I recommend eating vegetables rather than grains and potatoes. Eat broccoli with meat rather than rice. Eat asparagus with chicken rather than mashed potatoes. When you use vegetables as your main carbohydrate intake, you will eat them enough to increase your testosterone levels.

Eliminate Refined Sugars

Testosterone decreases after ingestion of white sugar. Glucose solution given to 74 men decreased blood levels of testosterone by as much as 25 percent, regardless of whether they had diabetes. Two hours after glucose administration, the testosterone level still remained much lower than before the test in 73 of the 74 men.

Eliminate Grains

Grains are not only the cause of belly fat which lowers testosterone, gluten in grains causes intestinal inflammation and often blood sugar swings so your adrenal glands are forced to overproduce cortisol. Once you over-produce cortisol, your adrenal glands won't produce enough sex hormones, which will often dramatically decrease your testosterone.

Grains are also in almost every modern commercial food usually mixed with refined sugars. So once you eliminate grains and refined sugars, you will eliminate most of the bad stuff. I know it's hard but at least start with eating brown rice or buckwheat rather than spaghetti or bread. When you also do intermittent fasting to decrease the amount of meals you eat, you will be able to do it.

Do Intermittent Fasting

I will write a whole book about it later on. Intermittent fasting is proven to not only boost your testosterone but to dramatically increase your human growth hormone. I do this myself and find it the easiest way to stay shredded and horny. I recommend you to not eat at least 20 hours, and eat correctly in 4 hour window in the evening. If you workout in the morning, don't worry about about eating before or after a workout, it's scientifically proven that protein timing doesn't matter in muscle gains.

Avoid Harmful Chemicals

Since one of the main reasons why our testosterone continues to drop year after year is the radical amount of chemicals in our air and food. Phthalates and paragons in most personal care products like lotions and shaving creams. BPA that is found in plastic bottles, plastic food packaging. Pesticides found on common fruits and vegetables. Get a stainless steel water bottle. Buy natural deodorant, toothpaste, soaps, shampoos and body wash that are Phthalates and paragons free. Stop smoking no matter what. Eliminate alcohol and caffeine as much as you can. Do not use antidepressants, cholesterol drugs, pain relievers.

Have sex

Just having an erection is enough to circu
throughout your body. Having regular sex
keep your endocrine system stimulated and
test levels. In turn with increased test levels, _
more sex. This Is truly a win-win situation. Hav   ..at-
ter what. Don't be choosy. A sex with an averag , even a fat
girl is better than masturbation and it will open your doors to
better girls. Put your ego aside and have sex with whoever you
can find rather than masturbating.

Relax

A study showed that after only 1 week of 5 hours or less sleep,
men showed a drop in testosterone of 10-15% and increase in
stress levels by 30%. So don't skip out on your sleep, aim for at
least 8 hours. On top of that, try to get the deepest and restful
sleep you can get.

Workout

It's been proven that lifting weights can give you a 40% boost
in free testosterone levels. You have to stick to fewer reps
with heavier weights. Also you have to incorporate all of
the full body compound movements into your routine. These
movements pump surges of testosterone through your body.
These movements include the deadlift, squat, bench press,
pull ups, and military press.

Avoid Stress

Being overstressed causes your cortisol levels to surge, sup-
pressing your natural ability to produce testosterone. In fact,
when researchers in a study found out that the male DPT students with an average age of 24 years had lower testosterone
than male athletes in their 50s. Best way to avoid stress is to
do what you are passionate about in your life. Another good
way is to avoid stimulants that create withdrawal cycles and
play with cortisol levels such as caffeine, nicotine and alcohol. Intensive workout and meditation is also great for stress
levels.

Tongkat Ali increases libido, increases your sperm volume and quality, makes your orgasms more powerful. D-Aspartic Acid helps your body convert cholesterol and its natural resources into testosterone. Ashwagandha significantly lowers cortisol and increases your testosterone levels. Magnesium and zinc alone can send your testosterone levels through the roof. Vitamin C reduces cortisol in your body so with less cortisol we'll produce more testosterone. Selenium is one of the building blocks for testosterone. Vitamin E, C and D are crucial vitamins for optimal testosterone levels. Take Tongkat Ali, Ashwagandha, ZMA and a good multivitamin daily for best results.

Eat Like a Caveman

The actual thing we have to tackle is our diet. Whatever problems we have with our diet today, as with monogamy, we can connect all these problems to agriculture and development of modern civilisations.

Human health took a severe hit from agriculture. The typical human diet went from extreme variety and nutritional richness to just a few types of grain, possibly supplemented by occasional meat and dairy after the finding of agriculture.

According to research, hunter-gatherer diet includes 78 different species of mammal, 21 species of reptiles and amphibians, more than 150 species of birds, and 14 species of fish, as well as a wide range of plants.

In addition to the reduced nutritional value of the agricultural diet, the diseases deadliest to our species began when human populations turned to agriculture. Today, thanks to modern civilisations, heavy metal, fluoride, chlorine, pesticides, dioxins and other dangerous chemicals that are in our food and products.

When James Larrick and his colleagues studied the still relatively isolated Waorani Indians of Ecuador, they found no evidence of hypertension, heart disease, or cancer. No evidence of anemia or common cold. No internal parasites. No sign of previous exposure to polio, tuberculosis, malaria. No erectile dysfunction and obesity. No low testosterone.

I say, in order to have high, raw sexual sexual desire, you have to start feeding like our ancestors. The way is to completely adapt caveman diet for once and for all. Caveman diet is another name for Strict Paleo diet or in women terms Keto

Diet(almost). It means eating real whole food while avoiding all processed and agricultural food.

It also means recovering from your addictions such as sugar, alcohol and caffeine. Here is the detailed list of what to eat and what to avoid.

Foods to Eat

Organic Meat: beef, lamb, chicken, turkey, pork and others. Eat organic. Conventionally produced animal foods typically contain hormones and antibiotics that are given to the animals to increase yield and fight diseases. When you consume these foods your increased estrogen levels will decrease your testosterone.

Fish and seafood: wild salmon, trout, haddock, shrimp, shellfish. Avoid farm raised fish at all costs. Don't be fooled by names like "Atlantic Salmon." While you might think that Atlantic salmon means the fish was harvested from the Atlantic Ocean, almost all Atlantic salmon is actually farm-raised.

Eggs: only organic eggs. Organic chickens are allowed to roam free and they eat worms and bugs which means their eggs will be richly yellow/orange and full of nutrition and free of crap.

Vegetables: broccoli, kale, peppers, onions, carrots, tomatoes, etc. You cannot really go wrong eating vegetables in any quantity. Vegetables will replace the grains and tubers you used to eat. When you go to a restaurant, you won't order a pizza or french fries, you will order steak and salad and you will be happy for it because this is your lifestyle.

Fruits: apples, bananas, oranges, pears, avocados, strawberries, blueberries and more. Fruits can be a great way to satisfy your carb-crazy body when you start eating caveman diet. In several weeks your need for sweets will vanish.

Nuts and seeds: almonds, macadamia nuts, walnuts, hazelnuts, sunflower seeds, pumpkin seeds and more.Every time you ejaculate, you lose what nuts have such as Vitamins B6, B12, E, Calcium, Magnesium, Selenium and Zinc. Nuts have most important stuff that boost testosterone production.

Healthy fats and oils: Extra virgin olive oil, coconut oil, avocado oil and others. When it comes to boosting testosterone, cholesterol is your best friend. Testosterone is literally made from cholesterol and without it you would have none.

Foods to Avoid

Grains: do not eat gluten-containing grains such as wheat, barley or rye. You will also need to eliminate oats, corn, rice, millet, bulgur, sorghum, amaranth, buckwheat, quinoa or any grain products like bran, germ or starch. Say goodbye to cereal, crackers, rice, pasta, bread and beer. Yes, beer. All grains are strictly forbidden on caveman diet. Read the book Grain Brain for details. If you will cheat then eat buckwheat or quinoa only. Don't eat grains.

Legumes: beans, chickpeas, peas, lentils, tofu, soy, soy-foods and peanuts. Legumes are not allowed in caveman diet because of their high content of lectins and phytic acid. Soybeans and soy products also contain a phytoestrogen that can lead to a rise in estrogen in your body, which in turn cuts your testosterone levels. If you will cheat then eat chickpeas or peas only.

Dairy: do not eat dairy products of any kind or in any form such as milk, cheese or butter. Caveman diet does not allow dairy products because caveman did not milk cows. Studies have shown that men who consume dairy products have high levels of estrogen which lower testosterone.

Sugar: do not eat added sugar in any form. That means no table sugar, brown sugar, molasses, agave, maple syrup or honey. You should also not eat artificial sweeteners in any form such as Splenda, Nutrasweet, Sweet n Low, xylitol or stevia because they are all processed.

Tubers: potatoes, sweet potatoes, yams, turnips, etc. Especially white potatoes are extremely high in carbohydrates. We tend to rely on them as a filling starch rather than eating more nutrient dense vegetables and fruits that are lower in carbohydrates and calories.

Processed Foods: Everything labeled "diet" or "low-fat" or that has many additives. Refined sugars and artificial sweeteners including stevia. Our ancestors didn't eat these foods. Plus, there is little argument in the scientific community that refined sugars and excess salt contribute to obesity, high blood pressure and heart disease.

Processed Oils: Soybean oil, sunflower oil, cottonseed oil, corn oil, grapeseed oil, safflower oil and other processed oil. They don't have enough omega-3s to compete with their abundance of omegas-6s. They are very highly processed and some types contain molecules that are destructive once cooked.

Caffeine: avoid caffeine because it disturbs your adrenal glands which make chemicals that help your brain to feel happy, strong, motivated and sexual. Stop drinking any forms of caffeine and you will see a huge gain in your wellness, energy levels and sex drive. It's extremely addictive so prefer only green tea if you really cannot quit. Read the book Caffeine Blues for details.

Alcohol: alcohol is a no-no. Beer is made from grains, and liquor also contains traces of gluten. Alcohol consumption increases production of an enzyme that results testosterone being converted to estrogen. Only exception can be drinking a glass of red wine only when necessary. Red wine contains resveratrol which partly prevents this conversation.

Tobacco: nicotine and cotinine in cigarettes inhibits and reduces testosterone production and produce toxic substances. The problem with tobacco is that it is extremely addictive. Once you are hooked you will be constantly messing up with your testosterone. Avoid at all costs. If you really can't, at least switch to vaping.

Workout for testosterone

I've personally trained many people and I have a well built body. I'm working out for more than 15 years and I have enough experience to tell you what you should do. What I will say will be about working out for testosterone. They are also all backed up by research you can do.

It's been proven that lifting weights can give you up to 40% boost in free testosterone levels and testosterone levels increase up to 50% with weight loss. However, it's hard to untangle which is the cause and which is the effect because high testosterone with increased muscle and decreased fat go hand in hand.

Resistance training to build muscle mass and lose fat elevates testosterone and reduces body fat and elevated testosterone helps build muscle and reduce body fat. After all, the short fact is, men who lift weights and has less fat has much more testosterone than men who don't.

Doctor Todd Schroeder is one of the world's foremost authorities on the relationship between resistance training and testosterone. He has found four factors for maximizing testosterone release with resistance training.

First, you have to train large muscle groups by doing compound movements. Second, you have to lift heavy weights with a 6 reps on average and no more than 4 sets for the whole muscle group. Third, You have to use short rest periods such as resting one minute between straight sets. Fourth, you should do cardio but not combine resistance exercise and cardio in the same session.

So, In order to optimize your testosterone levels for highest raw sexual desire, you have to do cardio and gain muscle mass. You need to do these at different times. You need to stress your body to get the biggest testosterone surge while getting enough sleep and rest.

When you take the correct actions inside and outside the gym, your muscles grow and you will lose fat. It's really that simple, and these laws always apply. These principles below have been known and followed for decades by people who built some of the greatest physiques we've ever seen. They are practical. Follow them consistently, and you will get results.

Rules of muscle growth

Train

What triggers muscle growth is overload. That means heavy weights, and short, intense sets of relatively low reps. In fact, a study of American College of Sports Medicine within hundreds of subjects, concluded that training with weights that allowed no more than 6 reps is most effective for increasing strength. Lift progressively heavy. Period.

Eat

Our diet determines about 80% of how you look. You could do the perfect workouts and give your muscles the perfect amount of rest, but if you don't eat correctly, nothing will happen. This is why eating Paleo and Intermittent fasting will make you look sexy. Forget about X gram protein calculations and protein shakes of stupid fitness industry. In your 4 hour eating window eat like a king, holding a big Turkey thigh in your hand. Eat lots and lots of meat with lots of vegetables such as broccoli, asparagus, etc. Then eat nuts, figs, bananas, whatever you like. Enjoy it. Don't count calories or proteins, fucking feast.

Rest

It takes the body around 4 days to fully repair muscles subjected to weight training. So you have to exercise a muscle group maximum once a week. Another aspect of rest is sleep since majority of your growth hormone produced during sleep. You should cut caffeine and alcohol that will impair your sleep and make sure you have to between 6 to 8 hours everyday.

Your Sample Workout Plan

When you combine consistent application of the above rules with the proper exercises, you can increase your testosterone production to the highest level by gaining muscle and losing fat.

I am now going to give you a nice training plan that works. It is designed to maximize testosterone production. This program can be a great start if you are a beginner or in the middle. If you want to go more advanced, subscribe to Greg Plitt's website. He teached supersetting low reps with high reps which also works great.

Monday: Chest
50 Crunches + 50 Russian Twist + 25 leg raises
Flat Bench Press – 3 sets, 12-10-8 rep warmup + 3 sets, 6 reps
Incline Bench Press – 3 sets, 6 reps
Decline Bench Press – 3 sets, 6 reps
Chest Dips – 3 sets, 6 reps
Dumbbell Flyes – 3 sets, 6 reps
Dumbbell Pullovers – 3 sets, 6 reps

Tuesday: Shoulders
50 Crunches + 50 Russian Twist + 25 leg raises
Military Press – 3 sets, 12-10-8 rep warmup + 3 sets, 6 reps
Behind The Neck Press – 3 sets, 6 reps
Upright Rows – 3 sets, 6 reps
Side Lateral Raise – 3 sets, 6 reps
Rear Deltoid Raise – 3 sets, 6 reps
Barbell Shrugs – 3 sets, 20 reps

Wednesday: Back
50 Crunches + 50 Russian Twist + 25 leg raises
Pull-Ups – 6 sets, 6 reps

Chin-Ups – 3 sets, 6 reps
Barbell Rows – 3 sets, 6 reps
Lat Pulldown – 3 sets, 6 reps
Dumbbell Rows – 3 sets, 6 reps
Back Extensions – 3 sets, 30 reps

Thursday: Legs
50 Crunches + 50 Russian Twist + 25 leg raises
Barbell Squats – 3 sets, 12-10-8 rep warmup + 3 sets, 6 reps
Barbell Deadlifts – 3 sets, 6 reps
Leg Press – 3 sets, 6 reps
Leg Curls – 3 sets, 6 reps
Lunges – 3 sets, 6 reps
Calf Raises – 3 sets, 20 reps

Friday: Arms
50 Crunches + 50 Russian Twist + 25 leg raises
Standing Ez Bar curls – 3 sets, 12-10-8 rep warmup + 3 sets, 6 reps
Dead Hang Curls – 3 sets, 6 reps
Hammer Curls – 3 sets, 6 reps
Tricep Dips – 3 sets, 6 reps
Skull Crushers – 3 sets, 6 reps
Triceps Pushdown – 3 sets, 6 reps

As you can see from the plan, it all consists of fundamental compound exercises. There are almost no isolation exercises, supersets, drop-sets, etc. 3 sets and 6 reps %95 of the time for maximal muscle growth. Lift heavy. Since sets are short, concentrate and focus energy on the heavy weights.

Start with abs which are the hardest. Warmup with 12 sets with half the heavy weight of the 6 rep working set. Then increase the weight for the 10 reps and 8 reps. For example if I do 120 lbs 6 rep 3 set bench press; I start with 12 rep 60 lbs, then do 10 reps 80 lbs, and 8 rep 100 lbs warmup.

Have training journal that you write your weights. Muscles grow by overloading. Every week try to increase the weight to make sure you are pushing yourself to the edge. Rest no more than 1.5 minutes between sets. Don't chat with anybody, don't try to meet with girls, listen to high bpm music and finish your training maximum in an hour.

I also take training off every 3 months since studies have shown that it takes a week for the central nervous system to fully recover from the stresses of weight lifting.

For cardio, I walk alone to meet with women or walk with your woman at least 1 hour a day.

Assignments

Approach 10 Women

Approach 10 women as I have written on day 1.

Write Your Daily Journal

Write your daily journal as I have written on day 1.

DAY 5 - CREATE RAW SEXUAL DESIRE | QUIT MASTURBATION

Why You Must Stop Masturbating

The reason you must stop masturbating is because you are short-circuiting your brain's reward system and thus handicapping your performance in many areas of your life.

Your brain is wired to seek out pleasure the fastest way possible. When you study for an exam and you put in the work, then you get a good grade, you obviously going to feel awesome. When you get the promotion at work, your brain will also reward you with some tasty dopamine. In both of those cases, you had to put a significant amount of work and effort to get the goodies at the end.

What would happen if you could get an instant pleasure at the click of the button? Well, you can do that by looking at porn and masturbating. You don't have to work for it, you don't have to approach hundreds of girls, you don't have to go through a string of rejections, you don't have to escalate. You just have to click a button.

What's wrong with that? You hook your brain on dopamine spikes and short term gratification.

Whenever you are faced with a task that requires a significant amount of time and effort, you can't focus anymore because it is nowhere near as rewarding, nowhere near as instantaneous as porn is. You reward yourself for being lazy. And your brain goes "hmm if I get dopamine when I'm lazy, then I guess I should be lazy".

On top of that, with masturbation and porn, you're tapping into the most powerful reward ever. What is the most powerful reward your body can give itself? An orgasm.

If you could attract any girl with just a click of the mouse, would you take the time to make yourself attractive? Your brain can't tell the difference between imagination and reality. This is why horror movies are scary even though there is nothing to be scared off.

You're wiring your brain to short term gratification and this becomes your norm in all areas of life. Your brain wants the cookie, but the problem is, that the more cookies you have, the less tasty they are!

All humans have basic drives. Drives are what makes us do things. <u>The strongest and most life altering drive in humans is their sex drive.</u> There have been many psychological studies proving this and if you think for a moment about why you do the things you do and say the things you say, you'll most likely realize that. That sex drive will cause a man to get a job, get out on his own house, be successful, and find mates.

Drug and alcohol abuse also short-circuits the brain's reward center same way as masturbation. Like masturbation, you naturally want to keep pressing the reward button to feel good.

So, if your reward system has not been altered than the reward system builds you up and helps you become a better person. However, when you release your chemicals unnaturally by an addictive chemical or by masturbation your reward system gets altered.

The problem is; <u>masturbation is a drug</u>. It has the same characteristics of every other drug. When you masturbate you are reaching for the pill instead of reaching for life. You are doing the same thing drug addicts and alcoholics do.

Sure it feels great and relieves the tension of sexual frustration. That's not the problem. The problem is that every time you masturbate you are doing a drug. The more you masturbate the more you are abusing the drug. The more you abuse the drug the more you alter your brain's reward system in relation to the sex drive.

And when you alter your sex drive you alter everything that is based on your sex drive. <u>Your ability to get women and make money</u>. Basically all a man wants.

Everything starts with natural laws. You might have heard of the opposites attract law. Electricity flows if there is a positive and negative charge. Masculine and feminine poles create a flow of sexual energy. Masculine men are going to be attracted to feminine women because they are on the opposite spectrum of the pole.

The more <u>polarized</u> you are, the stronger the attraction between you and a feminine girl, the more masculine the man is the more feminine energy he will attract. If you are depolarized, this will create a weaker polarizing effect.

<u>When you don't waste your sexual energy by not masturbating, you're positively charging your sexual energy and masculine polarity.</u>

If you let your sexual energy build up, you will become more masculine, more aggressive, driven, motivated and creative. A lot of men use their sexual energy as a source of their creative power and genius. This is also written in Napoleon Hill's Think and Grow Rich book as Sexual Transmutation. This is why throughout history man has always been more successful in every area than women. This is also why successful men have women behind them or do it to find women. This is why humanity advances. This is why capitalism goes on, etc.

If you're wasting your sexual energy though, you feel unmotivated, lethargic, and you take on more feminine traits. You will also feel less masculine. When you are masturbating, you keep depleting your sexual energy and never allow it to build up enough to experience the benefits of charged up sexual energy.

The Only Way to Quit Masturbation

The only way to quit masturbation is to have sex with real woman. Period.

Forget about Nofap, forget about willpower. Your reptilian brain's primitive desire for sex will always take over your control by overriding your logical reasons. It will always wear and tear your willpower. You will masturbate if you don't find sex.

Your question should be; "how are you going to delay masturbation until you find sex?". The answer is:

Be on the way to find sex with real woman.

That will give you the motivation to resist the urges for sometime.

Imagine you just established a company and you know that if you spend all your time this month on developing a certain feature of your product, you will get your first corporate client. Are you going to spend your time doing any other thing? No, you time constrained yourself for the aim.

If you put the time you sit at home and look porn to going out to meet with women, not only you will delay masturbation, but you will eventually find sex. If you don't do something to find woman, you will eventually masturbate. And when you masturbate you won't want to do something to find woman. It's a downward spiral.

Masturbation is like heroin addiction. In fact it does activate the same opioid receptors as heroin does. How do you quit heroin addiction? Can you do it by intellectualizing that heroine is bad by reading no-heroin forums? Never.

You have to replace the addiction with something else and ultimately learn get that pleasure from other things rather than the drug. That something else is real sex which is healthy. Your new addiction has to be real sex with women. Your way to reach that "drug" should be going out and approaching hundreds of women. Of course real sex can also destroy you but I'm talking about ultimately finding the woman you want to be with, not the quick sex you get on the way.

How to Quit Masturbation

When sex is not an option, you will have two choices when you are faced with the inner tension of sexual desire. You either masturbate and release that energy, or you transmute that sexual energy into other productive activity.

They are some emotions that you really don't want to feel. Financial problems, sexual frustration or feeling stuck in life. Just like alcohol and drugs, one of the most readily available coping mechanisms for these kind of negative emotions is masturbation.

We have been told not to show our emotions all our lives and we became such bottled up to explode. Masturbation is that explosion. Rather than getting angry, going out to the street, saying "enough is enough" and approaching 100s of girls with that energy, we numb ourselves to emotions in order to prevent ourselves from feeling bad.

And our brains get used to it. Next time, as soon as we start to feel the slightest negative emotion, we feel a natural inclination to shut it down, suppress and disconnect from it. This the root cause of every masturbation addiction, and actually every other addiction.

Alcohol, weed, cocaine, heroin, nicotine, caffeine. All of those substances temporarily alter your state of mind and bring relief from the emotion. However, every time you use them, there is a debt that will eventually have to be paid back. What goes up must go down. In this way addictions keep you stuck because they don't solve the problem, they just numb you away from it .

Emotions exist for a reason. We don't have to numb any of

them, instead, we have to learn how to process them. The problem is not the addiction, the problem is the suppressed emotional trauma, that is the cause of the addiction.

In a life free of your emotional baggage and insecurities, there would be no need to escape to any form of addiction. You could open up to anyone because there would be nothing to hide. The need to drink alcohol and use it as a social lubricant would disappear completely because you can relax and be social without it.

You can step out of your comfort zone fearlessly and approach that hot girl. The need to masturbate to cover your frustration would disappear because you would have real sex.

Anyone can develop that state of mind if they could remove the emotional blocks and allow the life force to flow. In order to do this, you have to process the suppressed emotions. There is no way around it. The only way is through it.

The first step is to stop masturbating completely and immediately. Don't ever tell yourself to do it one last time. Make the decision and commit now. Quit now and accept that next time a woman will do it for you. In this way you let your masculine polarity to grow and allow that energy to build up.

In a week, as the energy starts to build up, the more and more pressure will be put on those emotional problems. You will feel more and more inner tension and you will feel more and more uncomfortable. This is when most guys will resort to masturbating in order to relieve that pressure.

If you can resist masturbation though, then those suppressed emotions, as long as you don't suppress them with other addictions, will be pushed to the surface for you to deal with. At this point, you will come face to face with your inner demons. All the suppressed emotions will come up. These emotions are most like to be anger and frustration coming from your horniness.

Now, exactly at this point I want you to go out and start approaching women massively as if you are exploding. I want you to tell yourself "enough is enough, I will go out and find sex today!!". I want you to walk in the streets, go to bars and clubs, I want you to do everything you can to find real sex. Believe or not, every single time I found sex I was in that situation. I was sick of getting rejected, I was sick of being horny. I've put all my pain and anger into massively approaching and weeding out the women who don't want me so I could find the women (horny women) who want me.

In this way you can delay masturbation until you find real sex. Get up, go to work. Finish your work and start approaching women. Come home tired, eat and sleep. Do this every single day. Leave no time in between. If you do this, you will find sex and when you find sex masturbation will be history. You will feel the pressure for sure but don't give yourself a break, because that break may be the explosion of masturbation.

Pressure combusts pipes but it also creates diamonds. Think of yourself as a hunter who needs to eat. That hunger makes him go after the food. He may not catch today but he knows he will sleep hungry so he gives his all to today.

If you continue doing what I say and if you don't quit for several weeks, I guarantee you will find someone who is also horny and frustrated as you are and she will pick you up. You will also most probably amazed because horny and frustrated women are usually hot depressed women who get cheated by their hot boyfriends. You will be there to fuck her. She will pick you up because of your raw sexual energy and your vibrational match. You will find sex, quit masturbation and you will proceed to other girls with a better mindset.

Don't be choosy in any case. She may not be your perfect girl but what the heck? Is masturbation better than real pussy? Plus, you are teaching your brain to get pleasure naturally and this is your path to recovery and betterment.

In this way you will naturally quit masturbation because you will realize that quitting masturbation gave you what you currently have. Your brain will start to think; "hmm..that sex was better than masturbation, let's find out more about it."

You can either quit masturbation once for the rest of your life and face your demons, or you can continue running away from those emotions and come back to the road of addiction. I assure you that you will come back where you started when you just masturbate once, just like ex smoker taking a puff. However, If you choose to face your demons and conquer them, you will be free of the emotional blockage and masturbation will be history.

Assignments

Approach 10 Women
Approach 10 women as I have written on day 1.

Write Your Daily Journal
Write your daily journal as I have written on day 1.

DAY 6 - TAKE ACTION

Assignments

Approach 15 Women
Approach 15 women as I have written on day 1.

Write Your Daily Journal
Write your daily journal as I have written on day 1.

DAY 7 - TAKE ACTION

Assignments

Approach 15 Women

Approach 15 women as I have written on day 1.

Write Your Daily Journal

Write your daily journal as I have written on day 1.

DAY 8 - BECOME R-SELECTED | HUNGER

Psychological Attraction Mechanism

In surveys among thousands of women, there's one universal quality in men that they all find desirable. It's high social status. Where it becomes unclear is how women perceive status.

If we look at the research, it focuses on wealth. However, I have many wealthy friends who can't seem to be successful with women. When you look deeper in the studies it shows that women are equally at attracted to men that they believe have the potential to be successful as they are to men who are already successful.

This would also explain why the starving artist has no trouble finding girlfriends to support him, and the college athlete can date models even though he can't afford to buy her dinner. Social status is actually perceived by how confidently you present yourself.

If you read any book about "game" or watched a pickup video, you will come across to the oldest term of "push and pull". In "game", push and pull is presented to people as the best way to eliminate neediness. Push and pull is giving the girl mixed messages of both "I like you" and "I don't like you" so that she will perceive you as high social status.

However, I repeated over and over again that if you want to have sex with a woman, you first and foremost have to purely desire her without any strings attached.

As you may understand, what I am telling is completely in conflict with what "game" tells. This is actually a paradox in the seduction community and many men face this when he tries to seduce a woman. How do you show her that you want her, while still remaining high status? Wouldn't a man of high status have these women come to him?

People think that if a high status man pursues a woman, he makes himself low status and therefore unattractive. But if a man never pursues women, then he never turns her on by his desire so he never gets laid. So what should a man do?

What men don't understand is the difference between her physiological and physical attraction mechanisms.

Let me start with physiological. Her physiological attraction mechanism activated by your confidence. The more confident you are, the more attractive she will be attracted to you physiologically. That's why she will attracted to your status.

Confidence is knowing that you are a valuable whether other people recognize it or not and expressing your desires, your ideas, your values, your interests without shame or inhibition. Women don't judge a man's status by the car he drives or how much he earns. Women judge status by his behavior, and the behavioral trait they judge is confidence.

A man who is rich has greater potential to make a woman feel secure and comfortable, but if his behavior shows that he won't, if he is not confident enough to give her what she wants, then she won't be attracted to him. A physically fit man will imply a better choice for her children, but again, if his behavior shows that he won't be able to raise them, then she will not be attracted to him.

This is how women's physiological attraction mechanism works. It is formed by society and it depends on security and comfort. If you want to psychologically attract high quality women, you need to have social status, you need to have confidence.

This also solves the paradox. A confident man doesn't care

how she will perceive her, he just goes for what he wants.

Physical Attraction Mechanism

There is another attraction mechanism that is more important and potent. That is her physical attraction mechanism that is formed by millions of years of evolution. It depends on her sexual desire. Her animalistic sexual desire that is managed by her reptilian brain which is hundreds of times more powerful than her logical neocortex.

If you have a raw, untamed, pure sexual desire for her and if you are expressing it clearly and in a sense so feels it, she will be attracted to you regardless of you have confidence. Regardless of your status. Regardless of your looks. Regardless of anything else. I talked about sexual desire in the past days. I will just explain the seduction process here.

When a man meets a woman he likes, there are three possibilities of seduction processes may occur.

In the first seduction, he may demonstrate that he is more invested in her than himself. In the second seduction, he may give her the impression that he's less invested in her than he is in himself. In the third seduction, he may demonstrate that he is actually less invested in her than he is in himself.

First one is the default state of most men and "Game" and "Dating" advice tries to change that. It's the guy so badly needs sex and love. He acts like a little dog of her. This is called neediness and comes from fake confidence.

Second one is about the "Game" advice out there for men. How to perform as a man of high status would. Getting into the role of an alpha man, pushes and pulls, DHVs, routines. This is not neediness but it's fake confidence.

Third one is about the dating advice out there for men. You don't have to memorize anything as the game guy does. Knowing what you want, being yourself, having integrity, looking for better relationships and emotional fulfillment is enough. This is about real confidence.

All of them work with different types of women, however almost in all of them you will end up as being the provider guy. What do I mean by that?

In the first seduction, the guy doesn't even realize or care about the quality of the girl, he loves her for the rest of his life, settles in a relationship and does whatever she wants such as marriage. This has happened to all of my friends who didn't cold approach.

In the second seduction, the guy eventually sleeps with low to middle quality girls because only they respond to what he does. Eventually he finds an upper-middle quality girl and settles in a relationship as her boyfriend or husband. This has happened to all of my friends who studied pickup.

In the third seduction, the guy doesn't even bother with lower quality girls and he sleeps with middle to high quality girls. However he needs sex and finding a quality girls is hard, after a long time of try and fails, he finally finds a high quality girl, and settles in a relationship as her boyfriend or husband. This has happened to all of my friends who came from rich families or who were too busy building their businesses.

So all these types of seductions work but they eventually commit or marry with the highest quality woman they can find and start providing for her. Providing means financing her and the kids for the rest of your life as well as accepting to only sleep with her for the rest of your life. You "provide" for your family.

That may be good for some people and actually we all need that, however, none of these seduction methods will give you lots of sex with variety of women constantly. None of these seduction methods will create your harem for free.

There is only one strategy that can create your harem for free. It addresses directly to woman's physical attraction mechanisms. It's R-selection.

R-Selection

There are two types of mating strategies in the animal king-dom: R-Selection and K-Selection.

R-Selection means rate selection. It means that a male will try to impregnate as many females he can in order to produce healthy offspring. R-Selected men focus on being lovers.

K-selection means quality selection. It means a male will ul-timately impregnate only one or two quality females. So he focuses all of his energy and resources on raising his offspring to carry on his genes. K-Selected men focus on being pro-viders.

Women treat these two types of men very, very, very differ-ently.

Women choose providers according to their psychological at-traction mechanism to fulfill her needs for security and com-fort. Women will shame them for being overly sexual. They want him to stay in his assigned role of being safe, non-threat-ening boyfriend or husband.

If a provider says anything outside of his social role, women will say things like "You can't say that; that's really rude." or, "Aren't you a little old to be chasing girls like me?". He may not necessarily be the nice guy. He may be a successful, rich, great looking dominant guy with a real confidence.

However, at the end of the day, he has to be the guy who keeps smiling, who goes out with her friends, who never cheats, who pays for the dinner and eventually who brings home the food. Regardless of whether he has real confidence, fake confidence, rich, poor or good looking; women perceive him as the provider guy.

An R-Selected man however, doesn't care about a relationship. Doesn't care about keeping the woman. He just cares about what he feels sexually for her at the moment. He implies that at the very start of meeting her. Woman talks with him knowing or feeling that.

R-Selected man is never jealous if she has a boyfriend or husband. He is never jealous if she sleeps with someone else while sleeping with him. He is not needy if she will respond well to him. He doesn't care what she thinks about him. He can boldly make his sexual or teasing comments, and regardless of what a woman says, he maintains his energy and commitment to his sexual desire.

He is very comfortable with high levels of physical touch and communicates a very deep level of sensuality by playing up to her sexual desires and making them comfortable with feeling naughty. R-selected man give a woman complete freedom and privacy.

The R-selected man is going for the sex "right now" so he has to make her hot from the initial approach. In the first 5 minutes of the meeting she knows that the R-selected man may fuck her in a moments notice in the closest public toilet.

Most of the women just want adventure. They want the guy they can be free to just release themselves with and feel wild and untamed. Some want consequence free sex. Some want casual relationships. Most of them don't know what they want.

An R-Selected man appeals to her hard coded physical arousal mechanism. He appeals to her reptilian brain, her animalistic desires, her deep emotions. These trump her physiological arousal mechanism almost all the time.

R-selected man gets laid a lot with different variety of girls. He may still get into a long-term relationship and he may not necessarily cheat on her, but he never gets into the role of a provider.

The boyfriend has to be of acceptable social status, usually has to be from the same social class, age group, ethnicity and style. The R-selected man only needs to be sexy. I said sexy, not attractive. The attractive boyfriend with real confidence has to be attractive in various areas such as sexyness, age, integrity, style, potential wealth.

The R-selected man is just about sex. She has sexual needs and if you can satisfy them she might take time out of her day to jump you before going back to her boyfriend or her boyfriend search. She might as well be your girlfriend. When you are R-selected, you can easily sleep with lower, middle and higher quality girls regardless of your class, race, age, wealth or style.

Party girls will sleep with you. Business women will sleep with you. Younger women with sleep with you. Older women will sleep with you. Artists will sleep with you. Girls who want casual consequence free sex will sleep with you. Tourists in town will have their adventure sex with you. Girls who want a daddy figure will sleep with you. Real estate agents will sleep with you. Married women will sleep with you. Women will cheat on their boyfriends with you. I repeat, regardless of your class, race, age, wealth or style every woman can sleep with you.

You will finally understand that <u>you do not need to get into a relationship to get sex.</u>

When you present yourself as a person who is great to get involved with, the girl first puts you in the category of boyfriend then thinks: "Do I want to get involved?" and decides. You'll go to lots of dates and you will find lots of dates go nowhere because her shopping list for a boyfriend is long and she has an equally long list of eager rival suitors for that job.

Think about it. If she is even just 6 out of 10, she will have at least 10 men every day she can choose from Tinder, Instagram, social circle, clubs, parties, work, etc. She will always try to choose the best of the best "boyfriend". If she is 8 to 10, then we are talking about 100s.

When you present yourself solely as the sex guy; the girl checks if you are sexy then thinks; "what would I lose if I get involved with him?". "We just met on the street, nobody knows about us, he is making me horny...what would I lose?". A fast sex without consequences actually requires a lot less compliance than a relationship.

Don't get me wrong. If you are R-selected, you can still make girlfriends from a girl you've slept with. Once you fuck her good, which you will once you start to sleep with lots of girls, she will be willing to stick if she is available.

How to Be R-Selected

Being R selected is not easy. It takes experience as well as emotional stability. It starts with the right mindset though. You are R-selected when you are the sex guy. No one else but the sex guy. You have to accept that. That means, you will accept loneliness and that's the hard part.

So how do you become the sex guy? Well, you put all your focus on getting sex but nothing else. Don't expect a relationship as well as age, class, culture or status in a girl. Expect just raw sex.

You are sexy when you are hungry. When she sees the fire in your eyes and feels the rock solid erection in your trousers, and you are going for getting her home and fucking hard today, then you are sexy. How do you put fire in your eyes and get a rock solid erection? You have to get hungry for sex.

R-selected seducer is not the guy who goes to clubs on the weekends to pickup women, nor the guy who wears a business suit and goes to dates. He never spends much money on clothes, doesn't go to dinner dates and never goes to high end clubs.

R-Selected man is someone who does his own thing. R-Selected man is who hustles alone everyday in the streets through wind and rain. He gets shit faces for hours until a girl finally chooses him. His sex drive is so high that he sometimes he fucks fat girls just to satisfy his hunger. He has personality flaws coming from his upbringing that drive him to master his natural desires. He's lonely and broken but he is solid like an oak tree.

R-selected man is always hungry and stays hungry even after a conquest. His hunger destroys his fear of failure. Does he have fake confidence? No. Does he has real confidence? Not exactly. What does he have? He has hunger. He doesn't care about confidence. He doesn't care about shit. He has to eat.

Your raw sexual drive is the first gear, real confidence is the second gear. They will get you going, but hunger is the ticket that will take you there. Hunger will drive you through it. Hunger will be your resolve. Hunger is the raw sexual drive in action. It is the force that locks you into a commitment, it fastens you to the outcome and you won't sleep at night until you achieve it.

Hunger is irrepressible. It's a desire so strong that when you don't get whatever it is you're craving, you're disturbed.

After getting a "No" from a girl who is almost ready to fuck; Real confident guy says "fuck her, I have respect for myself..I will go and meet with a different girl tomorrow, nothing is more important than me". The guy with fake confidence says "the routine I memorized didn't work, let me tell her some DHV's and see if she gives me IOI's so I can pull her home".

R-Selected man says; "damn it, I'm so fucking hungry, I want her so badly, I'm going to fuck her no matter what" and pushes again. R-Selected man has the basic confidence, he also has the sexual desire but most importantly, he has the hunger that eventually gets him a girl.

I recommend you to be R-selected. It's just a mindset shift and that mindset shift will help you immensely. Forget about the great relationship you will find and focus on the quick raw sex. This mindset will ironically find you a great relationship as well as lots of sex. Only when you develop a strong sexual relationship with a woman, you have created the platform for the connection that you can enjoy. When you give your freedom more importance than anything else, she will love you.

Assignments

Approach 15 Women
Approach 15 women as I have written on day 1.

Write Your Daily Journal
Write your daily journal as I have written on day 1.

DAY 9 - BECOME R-SELECTED | FRAME CONTROL

Importance Of Frame Control

Frame control is directly connected with your ability to maintain your masculine center. If you can project your masculine essence out to the world, you are exerting your frame on physical reality. I'm not talking about your raw sexual desire here. I'm talking about your identity.

If you're a boxer you may have the frame that you are the greatest boxer in the world. That's a frame. That's a way of seeing things and interpreting the world.

When a guy girl speaks with a girl and she gives him positive responses, he starts feeling himself better and better as she continues to give good responses. But once the girl tests him or unintentionally says something bad, his frame crashes and he gets angry. A guy with frame control would not change his state according to the reactions he gets from the girl.

Another example can be a guy makes a joke and the girl doesn't laugh at it. The guy gets serious and also doesn't laugh at his joke. A guy with frame control would be comfortable with it and laugh on his own joke.

A guy who is in control of his frame shrugs off women's attempts to throw him off-balance, deflects jealous friends interfering with his progress and never seeks validation from her. On the other hand, a guy without frame control bows down to woman's insistent demands, gets off-balanced by a woman's tests and constantly seeks validation.

Frame control is how you lead decisively, remain calm and attractive, and above all, get what you want. Idea behind frame control is sticking to your true identity to get what you want.

It is directly related to how you present yourself sexually from the outset. You present yourself to a women as a great guy to be involved with a great job, nice clothes, decent house and a car. A woman thinks you would make an excellent boy-friend.

You make a friendly conversation with her in the first date and in the second date you try to take things more sexual. However she expects a boyfriend candidate should not take things faster with her, so she doesn't respond to your sexual intentions. While you will never lose her by escalating, it will take more than you expect. If you have presented yourself as a casual lover, she would expect you to take things sexual in the first date.

The problem that most guys run into is that the expectations they set do not match the actions they later take. They don't hold their frames. This is why as an R-selected seducer you have to make it very clear to women about what you want very early on even it comes across highly sexual.

You have to gently but quite firmly state or imply that you don't want her thinking you are like other men who are going to wait around and chase her forever in the hope that something might happen. Because of this, women will know what you are about, and she will either go along with it, knowing full well the price of admission or she walks away, not being interested in the offer.

Good news is, when you're attractive and sexy and you're up-front about what you've got to offer, there will be a lot of women who don't want to walk away.

How To Control Your Frame

When you are dealing with a woman you must know you're the best thing that has ever happened to her. Until you know that and believe it in your gut, you will always struggle with frame control. If you believe that, you will naturally have the most outstanding frame control.

When she throws up reasons why she can't be with you, you've got to know that all reasons are bullshit and if she doesn't be with you, she is about to miss the best thing. And how do you get to the point where you know beyond the shadow of a doubt that you're the best thing that's ever happened to her?

You do that by getting results. Until you get results you can do this by brainwashing yourself into believing your own propaganda using mind reprogramming techniques at the start. As you get results you won't need any more programming.

We will be talking about reprogramming in the later days and it will take time to change your mind. Until then, knowing these principles and follow them consciously.

Set Expectations Beforehand

Set the right expectations from the onset. You can do things like opening direct, having a sexual vibe and qualifying her from early on. Doing these sets the frame that you're a sexual, confident man who's screening her hard; and if she sticks around, she's automatically accepts your frame. Otherwise, she'll decide on her own frame, which, if you were moving slowly and acting platonic, isn't going to be the frame you want her to have you in at all.

Know What You Want to Accomplish

Communicate to her what you want to accomplish. One of the

principle places most men lose in frame control is not knowing and communicating what, exactly, what they are trying to accomplish. If you are going to ask a girl to go to a bar with you, know why you want to do it -- is it to cheer her up or to move things forward with her? Are you after her phone number, or getting her your house the same day?

When she pushes back, that's because in her frame the thing that you're attempting to do doesn't make sense. So, you need to show her why it does. You might say something like "Come with me; I'm going to cheer you up." or "Let's go; we're heading somewhere quieter so we can talk."

Know You're Right

Once you propose or tell something, you're stuck with it, so make sure you get it right on the first try, because if someone challenges you on it, you've got to push it through. So if you tell something dumb like "all Americans eat excess amount of fast-food" and she says that there are many who eat healthy..you can't abandon the ship and still command her respect.

You must also not get into any debate or argument, your points must be stated with social grace. The instant you start arguing, you may have won the battle but you've undoubtedly lost the war.

Qualify Her

If you go into any interaction with a woman feeling like you need to impress her, you lose it from the start. You must be expecting her to impress you. Think you have a business idea and the investor who invests in similar ideas comes to your university, what would you do? You would try to impress him with your idea, right? That's why she has to impress you because you are the best thing that has happened to her.

Girls usually challenge guys by throwing shit tests by asking questions like "aren't you too old for me", just deflect her test and challenge back to her with a question like "What makes you say that?" or "Why do you think so?" ..then you can continue with qualifying her with "Hmm, that's interesting about you", "I suppose, if you say so then..."

Assignments

Approach 15 Women
Approach 15 women as I have written on day 1.

Write Your Daily Journal
Write your daily journal as I have written on day 1.

DAY 10 - BECOME R-SELECTED | PURPOSE

Find Your Purpose

Each man, in every age group finds himself in a state of dissatisfaction with life, of which the most pressing symptom is a lack of good sex. So he naturally tries to address that first and he swallows the "get laid today" bullshit marketing message of the pick up community, while making the minimum possible changes to his existing life.

The harsh reality is that failure with girls is part of a wider failure with life. Girls function like test of a man's way of living. If you love your life, have enough money, keep yourself in shape, follow worthwhile pursuits and then go approach a woman with desire, she will almost certainly give you a good response.

Our male brains are designed to instantly calculate the signs of value of a girl such as height, youth, hip to waist ratio, facial symmetry and then signal it to our conscious minds as sexual desire. We already have the intuition for which girls we like and which we don't. No amount of makeup or expensive clothing can fool us for long.

Similarly, women think like this. Their brains are designed to instantaneously calculate what is valuable to them. And we cannot trick them out of it, not for long.

<u>Only if you pass that scan she will care about what you say.</u>

The primary element you must have is raw sexual desire. Then comes your solid frame. Next important thing is the aura you exert from knowing and applying your life purpose.

Women are captivated by men who are caught up doing something better than themselves. Artist caught up painting pictures, college athlete caught up playing in NFL, businessman caught up in building business, programmer caught up creating an apps or politicians swept up in campaigning.

All these men have life purposes that are bigger than "Mrs. Right." All these men put their missions on a pedestal rather than putting her on a pedestal. They may still get hurt if a woman leaves, or rejects them, but when all's said and done they have more important things to do.

Women love that. They absolutely love it. R-selected man knows his purpose in life. That's the only way he can keep himself emotionally stable.

Most of us have no clue what we want to do with our lives. Even after we finish school. Even after we get a job. Even after we're making money. It's a struggle almost every adult goes through.

Everybody says that we were each born for some higher purpose and it's now our cosmic mission to find it. I think this is a kind of shitty logic.

Here's the truth. We exist on this earth for some undetermined period of time. During that time we do things. Some of these things are important. Some of them are unimportant. And those important things give our lives meaning and happiness. The unimportant ones basically just kill time.

So when people say, "What is my life purpose?" what they're actually asking is: "What can I do with my time that is important for me?" This is an infinitely better question to ask. So ask this question to yourself; "what can I do with my time that is important for me?". The answer is your life's purpose.

When you know your purpose, it helps you differentiate between the important and unimportant. When you pursue your purpose, your life becomes filled with direction and meaning.

As opposed to wasting your time in a job you don't love, now you can work toward a career that better fits your purpose. As opposed to being around toxic people who are incompatible with you, now you can find people who share the same values to build your highest life. As opposed to living a random existence, now you can create your life of the highest meaning. Same with women. You will be with who truly wants you and weed out those who don't.

Define Your Cause

In the book Denial of Death, Ernest Becker discusses something called a "heroism project." He states that man consciously or unconsciously works on in the hopes of making himself immortal.

A heroism project can be anything from an old man writing a book to be remembered or a man creating a company with his name. According to Becker, mental illness, such as depression, comes when one's heroism project is failing. When you begin to believe that you are not making a difference, depression and defeat sets in.

Becker states that to be emotionally and mentally fulfilled, we all must have a heroism project that we make a contribution to some great cause we believe in. That cause must become so important to you that you have to risk everything you have for the service of that cause.

Whatever it is, there's some way you want to change the world and make it better, whether you know how to do it right now or not.

Ask these three questions to yourself. What makes me angry that it's so, that I think needs changing? Is there a valid reason why things are this way, what is that reason? Why are things the way they are, and how do I change that?

What you want to look for is structural problems, rather than people problems. People slip into whatever structure they're presented with. If you spend your time getting mad at people for not doing what you think they should do, you'll be wasting your time.

Instead, figure out why the current structure pushes them toward that behavior, and determine what would need to change in order to influence people to change their behavior.

For example, in writing this book, I never try to change people because I know that people never change. The problem is not the approach anxiety of men. Problem is the society that conditions a man to internalize that approaching a stranger women for romantic interest is weird.

According to society a man should go with social circle and online dating route. However, these routes expose him to such low quantities of women, he eventually settles with an average. Men are conditioned to do what society imposes on them and this creates the fear; this creates the approach anxiety.

The problem is men don't know that there is world full of sex out there if he tries. He doesn't so he can't discover that because he doesn't know how to overcome the fear society imposed him. Men don't have good strategies to deal with that.

In writing this book, my cause is to teach these strategies and encourage men to face their fears and change their mindset. I have other causes too and in other areas of my life I do similar things that by creating websites, providing housing, etc.

Find your purpose, have your causes. Ask those questions again and look how I found my purpose and causes. Once you clearly define them, forget about anything else and commit yourself as your life depends on it.

Never Make Her Your Purpose

Once you have a purpose you care about, you need to make sure it isn't derailed by you, neglecting your foundational purposes. I talked about the different parts of the brain in the introduction. Your reptilian brain will always win over your mammalian brain and neocortex.

If you have a purpose of creating a business that will change the world; that business must provide a shelter for you to live, food to eat and woman to have sex with in the first place. That business has to provide social relationships with your coworkers in second place and the joy you get from achieving your purpose in the last place.

If you address all of those first, your reptilian and mammalian brains will leave you alone to bring your higher level logically-selected purpose to reality. This is the reason why meeting with women or a woman must never ever be your purpose. Your purpose; your business let's say, has to be your purpose that enables you to get better quality women(sex), shelter, food, etc.

There is a real danger that woman being your purpose. If you already have your shelter, your reptilian brain will always seek sex as the primary thing. Especially when you get good at cold approaching you start to get addicted to it. That happened to me in my 20s and caused real financial trouble. I realized and fixed that. If that happens to you, if you make a woman or meeting with women your purpose, you will greatly suffer. Not only you won't have enough food and shelter, you will be extremely needy.

Many men think that whenever he finds a woman, he will give her absolutely the best relationship she could ever imagine.

He goes out to fill his purpose to find her. Sarging. Gaming. Daygaming. Night Gaming. Tinder gaming. Whatever the fuck they name it. You must never ever attach too much energy on learning pickup, getting responses, getting good with women or getting a woman. R-selected man never does that. Because when your purpose is the meeting, having or keeping a woman; this is the most repulsive vibe for women to feel. The worst of all.

It is a desperate man's bargain – because the resource is so very scarce, he says that he will do everything in his power to hold onto that resource once he finally have it in his hands. Yet, while women would certainly like to have a dependable men who will be there for them in need, they don't want to sleep with these guys in million years.

A woman want the best men she can get and that doesn't mean men who make them their primary mission whether it is for sex or relationship. Because a man who's going to make his woman his primary mission is a man without a purpose.

Each man seek a purpose to affix themselves to and most of them finding no greater purpose to pursue, they attach themselves to their lovers or finding a lover. When she leaves... it's devastating! The center point of your life is now, just... gone! This actually isn't something you can easily emotionally control.

Effectively, whatever you devote the greatest amount of emotional resources to becomes the emotional center point of your life. When a millionaire breaks up with a woman, he won't break down because his center point of his life is his business, not some women. When an artist breaks up, he won't because the center point of his life is his art, not some women.

But when your friend John breaks down after his wife leaves

him, he becomes a tearful, a bitter man for weeks and months on end. And you can sort of understand. After all, John has a shit job and mediocre friends. That girl was the best thing he had.

It is pathetic. That's why you need an emotional center that is stronger and more important to you than a woman or meeting with women The way to find that emotional center is having a purpose. That will solve the emotional emptiness of being R-selected.

A woman wants a man who's already on a mission for his purpose; whose life is consumed by his need to do something greater than himself and her. Forget all those romantic cliches of the leading man proclaiming his undying love for the woman who completes him.

Despite whatever protestations to the contrary, women do not want to be "The One" or the center of a man's existence. They in fact want to commit themselves to a worthy man's life purpose, to help him achieve that purpose with their feminine support, and to follow the path he lays out. This is the same story for same day lays as well as life long relationships. This is leading her.

"If tomorrow doesn't happen, would you still do what you're about to do today? If that answer is no, you're alive, but you're not living". Define what would you do for the rest of your life, find your purpose in it, define your causes and join you in your mission.

You will just be happy having her as a part of this great adventure of yours.

Journey Brings Us Happiness

R-Selected man sees life as a journey, because "journey is what brings us happiness not the destination".

Society teaches us that happiness is an emotional response to an outcome. "If I win I will be happy if I don't I won't". They taught us that happiness is result reliant. This is why we cannot sustain happiness because we immediately want something more when we get something.

If a good response from a girl or sleeping with her will define your happiness, then you are going to be let down frequently and be unhappy much of your time. The reason is because 95% of your time, you will get rejected.

I used to have a very beautiful and highly feminine girlfriend when I was 22 for a year. For long years after a hard breakup, I couldn't find someone like her. I couldn't feel anything with the girls I found after her and every rejection from girls like her was such a pain for me. It was an endless search and it was making me more and more bitter and unhappy.

It was pathetic. I knew I had to stop it, but I didn't know how. One day I read a book. It was called Peaceful warrior. It was after reading that book I realized the mistake I make. The mistake was attaching my happiness to an end result. Happiness by finding someone who responds me. Happiness by getting a date. Happiness through sleeping with a new girl.

I decided to stop attaching too much meaning on the result and started giving importance to the process.

As soon as the process of finding that girl, the opening and escalation became the reward in itself—I got more responses, more dates and more sex than I'd ever had before. I started enjoying the process. I wasn't thinking whether I will sleep with her or not, I was thinking all those little steps that will progress to something I could never know.

Emotional control is the foundation upon which all your interaction with a woman rests. You may be very horny and hungry but if you can't control it, you will lose it. You may have the greatest frame but if you get into argument you will lose it. If you come up with a dreadful vibe about your life, she will instantly feel it and you will lose it.

By mastering your emotions you can direct your outward vibe, which will in turn align the numerous subconscious behaviours that a girl's hindbrain unconsciously reads.

Good subconscious behaviours leads to imprinting the woman with a positive intuitive assessment of you, which will lead to smoother interactions both during the opening and escalation. This is why some men can have almost bad conversations and still get the woman because they were excelling at the 90% of communication that is non-verbal.

The key to mastering your emotions is being happy. And if you want to be happy, you cannot define your happiness by the end results. Happiness is something you find on the way, on the process. Even Tony Robbins says "progress makes us happy".

Feelings change. Sometimes sorrow, sometimes joy, sometimes anger. But beneath it all life always perfectly unfolds. Life is a journey and life happens for you, not to you. Everything happens for a reason. Everything helps you to tap into the person you truly are.

When you believe that all of the events, all successes and failures are all happening for a reason, everything works in your favor. The failures that used to break you and depress you only make you stronger and happier while successes you attach yourself to make you understand where you come from.

So if you want to be happy, see life as a journey. R-Selected man sees the life like that. Focus on the process and on the way I guarantee that you will be happy and no woman, no set back, no failure will be able to break you.

Assignments

Approach 20 Women
Approach 20 women as I have written on day 1.

Write Your Daily Journal
Write your daily journal as I have written on day 1.

DAY 11 - BECOME R-SELECTED | VULNERABILITY

Vulnerability

R-selected man is vulnerable. And that's his real strength.

Vulnerability is having the courage to show up and be seen when you have no control over the outcome. Just like you cold approach women every day. Vulnerability is an act of courage because you merge with your authentic self, instead of hiding behind a character to please others.

It is within the unknown where your greatest potential lies. Human nature is imperfect, yet the paradox is that we are whole within that sphere of imperfection.

Think of two men. One looks people in the eye when he speaks to them. Says what he thinks and he is comfortable if someone disagrees with him. He's not afraid to express his emotions, even if that means he gets rejected because of them. He has no problem moves on to people who like him for who he is. When he makes a mistake, he accepts it and apologizes if necessary. When he sucks at something, he admits it.

The second man is unable to look someone in the eye without getting uncomfortable. He puts on a cool persona. He dresses to show off. He performs. He avoids saying things that may upset others, and sometimes even lies to avoid conflict. He's trying to impress people. When he makes a mistake, he tries to blame others or pretend it didn't happen. He hides his emotions and will smile and tell everyone he's fine even when he's not. He's scared to death of rejection. And when he is rejected, it sends him angry and he tries to find a way to win back the affection of the person who doesn't like him.

Which man do you think women will be attracted to?

<u>If a man has problems with women, it is because his inability to express his true intentions to a woman.</u>

Maybe he has a set of limiting beliefs on how men and women should meet. Smiling at strangers makes him feel creepy, and the idea of hitting on a woman cares him because of the possibility of rejection. Perhaps he is afraid to talk with women he finds attractive. Perhaps he doesn't assert his sexual desire enough. Perhaps he is stuck in a job or lifestyle he doesn't truly enjoy.

All of these are symptoms have one problem in common; inability to make himself vulnerable.

Vulnerability isn't approaching a girl and telling how your ex-girlfriend cheated on you and dumped you. <u>Being vulnerable is having the courage to put your true self out there, your true intentions.</u>

Some guys will approach girls half-heartedly. Because if they get rejected, the idea that they only committed a half-hearted effort will soften the blow. Ironically, with this approach, the chance of rejection is sky high.

On the other hand, guys who show vulnerability will never put in a half-hearted approach. They put themselves out there 100% of the time. It's more of the: "This is who I am, and this is what I believe in. I've got strengths, but I've also got weaknesses. I may not be that rich or good looking but I'm doing my best to get better. I really like you and so badly want you. I deserve to be with you. I'm going to get you and I will be the best thing that will happen to you. You can either take it or leave it". When you go up to a girl like this, and she rejects you, be happy because she is really not the person who is going to make you happy anyway.

When you're vulnerable, you put yourself in a position to potentially crash and burn. And if that does happen, you're perfectly okay with it.

Vulnerability has a genuine feel to it, and women are instinctual when it comes to determining whether you're bullshitting or whether you're being genuine. Vulnerability is attractive because it's also a true indicator of confidence and being socially high status. A high status man has a set of values that he firmly believes in such as: "This is who I am, and this is what I believe in". He is not afraid to show his emotions and intent. If he's in the wrong, he'll admit it without much hesitation. He won't hide his weaknesses.

On the other hand, a low status man will do anything for approval. He hides his emotions and intent. He doesn't have his own set of values; he adheres to the values of the group. But if he's in the wrong, he'll come up with a lame excuse or shift the blame to someone else.

To be vulnerable with a woman is to allow yourself to be seen and known with your weaknesses, not just your powerful self. Yes, you are the most incredible thing that happened to her but that doesn't mean you are perfect.

To be vulnerable is to show her your fear, pain, shame, and maybe need for love. Showing your vulnerability is showing your weakness and therefore showing the way to be attacked. The opposite of vulnerability is keeping your protection from being hurt. Trouble is that also keeps all intimacy away from you.

It's often more difficult for men to show their vulnerability. We're taught to hold in our feelings. Most of the pickup advice tells us to hide our weaknesses and focus on strengths to conquer her.

Our ego desires us to be important, delusionally "high value". In reality, doing what our ego wants brings us only pain and suffering, because it makes us feel that we aren't enough as we are.

I say, "let go". Stop trying to be perfect. Expose yourself and share yourself without inhibition. Don't be afraid to reveal your sexual intent. Take the rejections, frustrations and move on because you're a strong man. And when you find a woman who loves who you are, leave yourself to her affection without caring the strings attached to it.

Sharing yourself openly with others forces that transition from that unconfident and afraid character who only cares about what others think to confident and comfortable person who cares how you feel about yourself.

Become comfortable with being imperfect. Being vulnerable forces you to accept and prioritize your own perception of yourself over those of others. You will get a "Don't Give a Fuck" attitude out of yourself that is genuine yet giving at the same time. You will know that you are the best thing that happened to her but also know that there is nothing to show off or hide from her.

This can only be done by consistently exposing yourself and opening up your sexuality, emotions and true thoughts first to yourself and then to those around you. The way to combat a lack of confidence and be a true R-selected lover is by opening up to your vulnerability.

Assignments

Approach 20 Women

Approach 20 women as I have written on day 1.

Write Your Daily Journal

Write your daily journal as I have written on day 1.

DAY 12 - BECOME R-SELECTED | ENTITLEMENT

Importance Of Entitlement

Do you believe in your gut that you are worthy of the hot women? R-selected man does.

Have you ever seen a beautiful girl walk by that is so amazing, so incredible that you couldn't think of what to say and you felt intimidated going up and speaking to her or your mind just went blank? If you have felt worthy of a girl, you would just be very relaxed and very chilled to go up to her like it's no big deal.

Fundamentally, there are 2 aspects to look at when trying to improve yourself with women. First one is, everything you do before you approach her. Second is, what you do after you approach her.

What you did before approaching her greatly influences what you will do after the approach. In such measures that the first aspect influences 90% of the seduction while second aspect does just the 10%. This is why men who don't read "game" theory or get dating advice still can get beautiful women.

Everything you do before the approach, the 90% part, includes first having sense of entitlement for her. Such as loving your life, having a fulfilling career, having a fulfilling social life, cultivating a positive mindset, going to the gym, eating right and most importantly, having an unapologetic raw sexual desire for her.

If the vast majority of this side of things are handled, chances are women are already entering your life and are probably already attracted to you. Maybe it's just a matter of putting yourself out there a bit more and maybe learning some techniques of how to approach and escalate more effectively.

The 10% part, what you do after the approach is less of the equation. If the first part is not yet handled to a sufficient enough degree though, then you can master the mechanics of the perfect approach and escalation precisely, and still not achieve what you want.

There are two stereotypes in the seduction community. The "natural" and the "PUA". The "natural" is simply a guy who has so much of the first part handled, that he doesn't need to ever work on. He's already there. He gets enough results that he doesn't need to put any effort into learning seduction.

Seduction is just something that happens when he's around a certain woman, some of the time. Kind of like making a new friend. How exactly could you study how to make friends? To him, the idea of learning a science of meeting women is just as absurd. It's just something that happens naturally when there's a 'spark' or 'chemistry' between two people, that's all!

The PUA is the exact opposite. Having never had success with women, he believes in theories that seduce models by simply following a few steps regardless of his desire, looks, wealth or social skills. And of course, for the most part, when a guy learns all the PUA theory and does it perfectly, he's only gotten 10% of the way there!

This is why most guys who get into PUA community never achieve the results they want. Because they keep believing that one new piece of theory will finally unlock their inner PUA.

When compared to PUA, the success of natural guy comes from his sense of entitlement so he can project his sexual desire easily. Most probably he starts feeling entitled to hot girls from his childhood so he gets results. After all, after every small success, we genuinely feel we deserve whatever rewards come our way. This is a big compound increase over the years.

So when he talks with a girl, he comes from countless past reference experiences he has and feels completely relaxed and in control.

Contrary to natural, PUA comes from lack of entitlement from his upbringing. Because of his flawed mindset, he cannot get results and rewards over the years, so his sense of entitlement decreases in a compound fashion.

This is the reason why while naturals getting girls more and more effortlessly, PUA puts more and more effort for less quality girls. Just like the rich get richer, poor gets poorer.

If I feel entitled to ownership of an object, I will simply walk over and pick it up, without hesitating, without asking anyone if it's ok, or minding what others think of my actions. Similarly, if I feel entitled to a beautiful woman, then I simply walk over to women I find attractive and introduce myself, say whatever's on my mind and escalate her. I don't hesitate to ask permission if it's ok to talk to her, or worry how I'm being perceived by others.

To walk up and perform a direct approach, especially on the street, and then also apply a rapid escalation; is labelled "bold" or "weird" according to many people. However, in reality it is nothing more than a by-product of a simple belief saying that "I am worthy of sleeping with attractive women so when I see an attractive woman I like I just go and talk with her and escalate to bed."

Conversely, the PUA learns the tricks and techniques, but even if he does get some success, often he finds it hard to get sex consistently or get into relationships he wants. Because when he sees the woman, he thinks and freezes.

It doesn't come from a primal gut feeling, it comes from the intellectual mind that society imposed him all through his life. Pickup content is just a part of it. At the end of the day, nothing changes his deep down feeling that he is unworthy of the attractive women.

Not every guy is a PUA and most of the guys are not naturals with women. However, where most guys fail is by raising the bar too high on what they "need" to feel entitled. At a deep core identity level they don't feel worthy enough for the kind of girls they like, and usually come up with "logical" reasons for this.

They either come up with a direct reason such as "I have no money" or "I am not good looking enough". They invent reasons why a sense of entitlement should no longer apply such as "I lost my job and I have no money anymore" or "I have gained too much weight".

These reasons may be real, and most of the time they are real. That hot girl really wants to go out with a good looking guy with a nice car and money in the bank. And you really may have a boring life, you may be average looking or you may not have much money.

However, what you don't realize is that girl, at some point in her life, did sleep with a guy like you. Maybe she didn't loved him as much or it was just about having sex, but at some point of her life, she slept with a guy who is no different than you. You also don't realize that she is usually wearing makeup, and maybe you would not want her if you have seen her in the morning.

First of all, many women are not better than you. They hide who they are behind makeup, sexy dresses and their inflated confidence value from social media. They never face the life as men face and develop as a result of it. If you really get the know most of the "hot" women, you would really look down on them.

Second; women don't necessarily need your money, especially if you are not looking to marry one of them. Being on the way to become the best version of yourself financially is enough. Women don't necessarily care how good looking you are. Trying your best to keep yourself in shape and dressing well is enough. Women are primarily looking for your behaviour. How you really and purely want her and the degree which you live life on your terms and is happy with it.

What is attractive to them is your sexual desire, your character, lifestyle and your outlook. If you're living life on your terms, exactly the life you want to live, even without having money, that is attractive to them. Otherwise no poor artist or aspiring businessman would get any girls.

You just need to take care of the fundamentals in your life and never let your finances, your look, or any other temporary situation prevent you from meeting women. You still have your character – that is what women respond to. It is all you ever really have. It's how you feel entitled to beautiful women.

Follow Your Instincts

When you see a woman you like, you must not think, but go get her with your instinctive raw sexual desire. Having raw sexual desire for her will shut your intellectual mind and your reptilian brain will take over.

When you intellectualize the situation, a negative thought will come up no matter how you good you are or how many experiences you had. Let your sexual desire take over your control and take you to action.

Take Action

Your entitlement is fluid. If you are sitting on the couch, not working on your purpose, not working out, not eating right and masturbating; your level of entitlement will go down. But if you take action like working on your purpose, working out, going up there and talking to girls consistently, your entitlement will go up. You will eventually build momentum. You will eventually quit masturbating. You will eventually build that sense of entitlement for better and better girls.

The World Owes You Nothing

Average men see other average men walking around with stunning girls, and feel deeply angry that they are not with a stunning girl. They see themselves as his equal, even as better and unique than him and they secretly wonder if they are lacking in one area or another, but never admit that to themselves.

Instead they insult the man or woman and complain instead of working to improve themselves. This is insecurity and jealousy. If a girl chooses to be with you, she has very specific reasons as to why she is with you, even though she is not aware of them. This is the same for you, you want to be with her for specific reasons. Both parties get something from each other.

In your case; you want to get a partner to get sex, a companion to be fulfilled emotionally, or a potential wife if that's what you want. In her case, she wants to get a lover to have great sex, a strong man to protect her or a provider to care the household. These are some of the factors among many and if you don't one or more of these qualities, you simply don't have enough value to attract her.

If you ask a guy why he should be with a certain girl, he will often begin by saying: "I'm really good guy". Unfortunately, nobody cares if you are a "good guy" unless you have something more to offer. People only care about what you bring to the table to fill their needs. If I need a custom made suit, am I going to find a good guy who says he can do it or am I going to find a tailor? If a woman wants to have great sex, is she going to have sex with a man who will "try really hard for her" and "be really nice," or will she go for the guy who can give her orgasms?

Focus on giving the world what it needs to get what you want.

You are not a Snowflake

You entitlement to her should come from your desire, not from your uniqueness or betterment. That's why I am saying that raw sexual desire is the most important thing you can have.

How I visualize entitlement to be in action, is where you don't think to yourself intellectually "Of course I can fuck that girl", but you just see her and want her, that very pure sense of just wanting.

Entitlement isn't about knowing you can have her, or you are better than her, or you deserve her. It's about the instinctive feeling.

Knowing happens in your brain, not in your balls. When you instinctively feel you can have her, you're engaging with it on a primal level and those logical thoughts are going to shut down automatically. Feel entitlement in your dick not in your mind. When you're hungry and see food, you just want the food. You don't think, "Am I entitled to this food?", you go and get it.

Assignments

Approach 20 Women
Approach 20 women as I have written on day 1.

Write Your Daily Journal
Write your daily journal as I have written on day 1.

DAY 13 – CHANGE YOUR PROGRAMMING | YOUR BELIEFS

Meet Cus D'Amato

Cus D'Amato is the man who is responsible for moulding Mike Tyson into the fighter that he became.

When Mike met Cus at the age of 13, Cus filled his head with philosophy; "I don't care how big or strong you are, if you don't have the spiritual warrior in you, you'll never be a fighter". Cus would speak to Mike about his mind: "Your mind is not your friend Mike, I hope you know that. You have to fight with your mind, control it".

At the age of just 14 Mike became a true believer in Cus's philosophy. He knew that if he wanted to become heavyweight champion of the world, he had to start living the life of one. He said "Always training, thinking like a Roman gladiator, being in a perpetual state of war in your mind, yet on the outside seeming calm and relaxed".

Cus had Mike repeating the words "I am the best fighter in the world. Nobody can beat me" over and over again. <u>If you repeat something to yourself enough times, you will eventually believe it</u>. Mike was given a mission by Cus, to become the youngest heavyweight champion of all time. Mike said "This is no joke, this isn't fighting for trophies, this is fighting for destiny".

At night Cus would come into Tyson's bedroom while Mike was in bed and repeat his affirmations to really sink them in. D'Amato built Mike's confidence and ego until it was towering above all opposition. Cus said to Mike "You're so superior to those people. They can never do what you are capable of doing. You could conquer any world. You are a colossus among men".

Cus was removing all doubts from Mike's mind and building his self-image to grandeur. Mike Tyson said; "I look at boxing as 90% psychological...the physical side has very little to do with it, if anything". Most people view boxing as a very physical sport. According to Tyson his success "was all psychological".

Mike was reading books about history's greatest warriors; Genghis Khan, Alexander The Great and Achilles. He would regard himself as being just like them. He said this was the only way to become great. You have to believe you're greater than you actually are. "Fake it till you make it".

The idea of believing you're the best is used by champions across many sports. But Mike was extreme: "I wanted to be Achilles right then" he said. Looking back at those days, he now declares that he was a "sick megalomaniac".

Adding to Mike's psychological weaponry, Cus took him to a hypnotist. His therapy included: "You are the world's greatest fighter". Tyson used visualization techniques, created by Cus D'Amato, to help him see himself as a fierce, quick-footed boxer.

Cus had Tyson engage in visualizations as part of his nightly ritual. Occasionally, Cus would sit next to Tyson's bed and assist him with his nightly visualization routine.

Cus had Tyson visualize himself as the undisputed heavyweight champion of the world, a fearsome, unbeatable fighter and as one of the best boxers of all time, even better than Marciano and Ali. He had him visualize his training and his bouts. Cus turned Tyson's brain into a virtual movie theater.

Affirmations were another part of the reprogramming techniques Cus used on Tyson. Cus had Tyson repeat various affirmations that were tied to his goals, in bed. Cus would repeat many of the affirmations to Tyson even during the day, just before falling off to sleep and when he was sleeping.

He'd feed Tyson's mind with statements about being unbeatable, becoming the undisputed heavyweight champion, going down in history as the greatest boxer the world had ever known, etc.

Part of Tyson's training regimen included repeatedly hitting a torso displayed on a mattress, over and over again in the same specific spots. Every combination he threw at that mattress became programmed into his subconscious. This soon became a habit that Tyson would take with him into the ring. After a fight Cus and Tyson would go over all of his mistakes, and then correct them in the gym.

Starting from Mike's amateur days, Cus viewed every one of those fights as a learning experience for Tyson. Cus told Tyson that the best lessons came from being defeated. That's where the hard lessons were learned, he'd tell Tyson.

Mike Tyson would really believe that he was the best boxer ever before he has ever won a match. Once he's beaten every other contender, his frame control became unshakeable. The result was supernatural confidence and God-like authority in the ring. There was no way another fighter entered that ring against him with as much purpose and self belief.

All that training carried him right to his life goal: he became heavyweight champion of the world aged just 20 years old. Mike Tyson was the product of an intensive <u>brainwashing regime</u> that transformed him from a street thug into a boxing legend.

If you want to be a Mike Tyson in your life, you have to reprogram your reptilian brain with the sub communications of the right frame. So you will take the actions with the right frame of mind. You don't need to go into hypnosis. You do it by

<u>repetition</u>. You do it by affirmations, visualisations, self talk and most importantly; real life results.

How Your Beliefs Are Created

Life is not a matter of luck or fortune. We are not playing our lives out at a gaming table. If we leave our lives up to chance, chances are, we'll fail.

If something happens to you; it happens because of something you created, directed, influenced, or allowed to happen.

In most cases, if you do the right thing, you're going to achieve the right results. If you like your job, do the right thing at the right time, and keep at it, there is a good chance that your job will do well for you.

If, on the other hand, you do not like your job and do things which work against you on the job, it won't work as well for you. How you manage yourself, what you do, how you act, each and every moment, every word you speak, motion you make, and action you take, or do not take, will determine how well anything in your life works for you.

But why do we do what we do? What makes us do what we do? What makes us act the way we act, behave the way we behave?

Remember the last you broke a promise you gave to yourself. The reason we don't even listen to our own advice is because of something else which affects, directs, influences, or controls all of our actions. That something that makes us do what we do is called our feelings.

Every action we take is first filtered through our feelings. How we feel about something will always determine or affect what we do and how well we do it. If we feel good or positive about something, we will behave more positively about it. Our feelings will directly influence our actions.

Have you ever watched a child who was made to eat something he didn't like? How did he act? But set a favorite dessert in front of the same child and what will he do? It's not that one type of food is better than the other. The difference is in how the child has come to feel about the food.

Your feelings about anything you do will determine how you do it. It doesn't have to be feelings of like or dislike, joy or fear; all of your feelings affect your actions. How you feel about your job, women, money, your health, yourself, your success, will determine how you behave in each of these areas. If your feelings are positive and productive, your actions will follow.

But what causes you to have the feelings Did you get them by accident? What creates the way you feel about anything?

Your feelings are created, controlled, determined, or influenced by your <u>attitudes.</u>

Your attitudes are the perspectives from which you view life. It's your world view. If you have an appreciation for women and you accept them as they are, your attitude towards women will be loving and affectionate. If you are angry and bitter towards women, your attitudes will be totally different.

Whatever attitude we have about anything will affect how we feel about it, which in turn determines how we'll act about it and that in turn determines whether or not we will do it well.

But where do you get your attitudes? Are you born with them? Or they just appear out of nowhere? Your attitudes are created, controlled, or influenced entirely by your <u>beliefs.</u>

What you believe about anything will determine your attitudes about it, create your feelings, direct your actions, and as a result, succeed or fail.

<u>Belief does not require something to be true. It only requires us to believe that it's true</u>. That means most of what reality is, to each of us, is based on what we have come to believe whether it's true or not!

That means, <u>we can create our reality with our beliefs</u>.

A young guy can believe that approaching women he likes in public is weird and rude. Another young guy can believe that approaching women he likes in public is completely normal and good for her. What they believe will completely affect their attitudes, feelings, and actions.

We all have thousands of big and little beliefs about ourselves. Some of them probably are true. I suspect that most of them are not. But your mind will act as they are true if you believe in them.

What makes us believe? Do our beliefs just come out of nowhere? Were our beliefs handed to us on the day of our births? Do we create them ourselves? do we get them?

<u>Our beliefs are created and directed entirely by our programming (conditioning)</u>.

We believe what we are programmed to believe. Our conditioning, from the day we were born, has created, reinforced, and nearly permanently cemented most of what we believe about ourselves. Through family, society, media, etc. we program ourselves.

Whether the programming was right or wrong, true or false, the result of it is what we believe. <u>It all starts with our programming!</u>

In logical progression; programming creates beliefs. Beliefs create attitudes. Attitudes create feelings. Feelings determine actions. Actions create results. That's how the brain works. If you want to change your results, you have to start with the first step. <u>You have to change your programming first</u>.

Affirmations

I won't go into detail of explaining what are positive and negative affirmations because chances are you already know them. Knowing is not enough though, you have to do. I know it's hard to repeat statements to yourself over and over again so we won't do that.

Most practical and effective way as also Bruce Lipton says is to create a script that consists of affirmations, then recording and listening it repetitively at night when you are sleeping. That's all, every night before you sleep, put your headphones or "sleep headphones" on and listen to it in a low volume while sleeping.

Tomorrow, I will provide you my affirmations so you can change them according to your needs.

Visualisations

I want you to visualise the person you want to become. Dwell on a vision of you being great. Dwell on vision of you accomplishing your goals. Dwell on an vision of you doing the things you want to do. Also dwell on a vision that you bleed and sweat when necessary to become the vision of yourself that you want to become.

Always visualise the end result and visualise it as it has already happened. Visualise yourself in the future exactly living your dream life.

For example, if you dream of having your own company and having a beautiful woman who loves you; then visualize a day that you are sitting in your company desk, she comes after work, you take her with your car to a restaurant. Visualise that day.

Tomorrow, I will provide you my visualisation scripts so you can change them according to your needs.

Assignments

Watch Video On How We Are Programmed
Please carefully watch video of Bruce lipton.
https://www.youtube.com/watch?v=7TivZYFlbX8

Watch Video On Sleep Programming
Please carefully watch video of Bruce lipton.
https://www.youtube.com/watch?v=X_MDb0HzFE0

Approach 20 Women
Approach 20 women as I have written on day 1.

Write Your Daily Journal
Write your daily journal as I have written on day 1.

DAY 14 - CHANGE YOUR PROGRAMMING | YOUR SCRIPT

My Affirmations Script

Below is my affirmations script. The first part is about how I live my life. This is my dream life. The second part is my beliefs. Note that beliefs have explanations. The reason is because I really want to remember why I can believe that affirmation.

The reason affirmations don't work for most people is because they don't believe in them. A guy affirms himself that he is rich but he neither earned much money before nor he has the reasons why he has the potential. You cannot hear your affirmation and tell yourself "yeah right". You have to really believe in them. So find those reasons and see the potential and write them as I do.

I have a document for my affirmations and visualisations. I read them once a week with their explanations just in case if I doubt any of them. When you record your script you will just read the italic texts.

Here are my most important beliefs about myself, women and about my dream that I live.

My Beliefs

I am a warrior - I won't settle under no circumstances.I will never be civilized. I will never get soft. I will show up today, tomorrow and years after. I will never arrive. I am always ready for isolation, rejection, self-doubt, despair, ridicule, contempt, and humiliation in area of my life.

I have to suffer - I know that all theory is bullshit. I have to go through hell.I have to put myself out there and fail over and over again to get what I want. If I am not good enough, I will make myself good enough. I expect disappointment before

1and. I have to suffer and persevere through it. That's how I succeed in any area of my life.

I am imperfect - I am aware of my own shortcomings and imperfections. I know that most of my attempts will be far from flawless. I will do stupid things, and fall far short of perfect. I accept that and know the fact that authenticity is more important than being perfect. I have nothing to hide. I accept my imperfection and do everything I can do to get better.

Cold approaching is natural - I slept with many girls through cold approaching. There are thousands of guys on Youtube who are doing it successfully. There are many sick people out there. There will be people who don't like it. They may laugh, yell at or threaten me. There may be girls who may not like it. There may be girls who may tell me that I am harassing or threatening them. I may get into fights. Police may stop me and take my details. At the end of the day, nothing is ever going to happen because nothing ever happened after doing more than 10000 approaches. The reason is because cold approach is completely natural.

It's all on me - Bet on yourself. You never lose if you bet on yourself. No one is helping me. No one is saving me. I cannot have a friend who helps. My family cannot help. I cannot have a coach. I have to do it myself. I have to go out there and take action. I have to motivate myself when I am down. I have to push through the resistance. Self discipline is everything. I will discipline myself by cutting any possibility of getting help. I cannot count on anyone including my friend, family or coach. If I count on anyone, I will be dependent on that person. I will succeed in all areas of my life without depending on anyone.

I will never be her boyfriend - I completely remove the idea of finding a girlfriend from my mind. I am out there for finding sex for the same day. I only have sex in my mind with this limited time frame. All I focus is fucking her and putting her in a rotation with other girls as soon as possible. I have to choose between being the provider or the lover. My intentions will create my reality. I choose being the lover. This is why I am enough for any woman because I am not aiming to be her husband or boyfriend, instead I am aiming to get quick sex from her.

All women are promiscuous - women will do all sorts of naughty things, act filthy, sleep with guys because they follow what their emotions tell them in that moment. This is why they often end up with totally unsuitable guys, hook up with bad boys who may treat them badly, and all sorts of other self-defeating behaviours. Girls have the hard-wired capacity to cheat but that doesn't mean they actually feel good about doing it. They'll often talk about being drawn to the bad boys against their better judgement. They'll often express regret at their illicit affairs and cry afterwards. I accept that and see it as the nature of women.

Woman love sex more than men - Women are more sexually voracious than men. Women love sex, they absolutely love it! According to research women love sex up to 3 times more than man. They have dirty and crazy fantasies that I cannot believe. They just do not want to be perceived as slutty. I know that it's very easy to land myself in that non-sexual bracket. That's why I never take things slow. I see any girl as a sex crazed slut, be unapologetically sexual and make same day lays my standard.

I can't be jealous - I am an R-selected man and I can never be jealous or show my jealousy. This is an agreement I make with myself before I start any relationship. Jealousy doesn't show that I really love her. It shows that I am afraid that she jumped in bed with another guy. That has nothing to do with love, but with deep-seated insecurity. If I constantly worry about whether she is cheating on me, she will cheat on me.

She feels what I feel - All humans, but especially women, have the ability to pick up on vibe. If I am feeling horny, confident, happy, relaxed, in control, and I talk with a woman who is on the same frequency, I will harmonize with her. If she is feeling down, fearful, or anxious, and my positive vibe is stronger, she will be compelled to tune into my vibe.

Attraction is not a choice - All women have dual mating strategy. All girls throughout their lives, even if they have boyfriends or married, pursue both high quality male DNA and long-term protection and provision. This gives my way in. Girls are hard-coded with the potential to step out on their long-term partners in order to access better DNA. They'll call it a "mistake" or an "adventure" but the important point is that it happens. They are never in control of their base impulses.

I am getting laid today - I always escalate. Fuck Day 2's. There is no tomorrow. I will bounce the girl for coffee and then bounce her to a bar and then back to my place. From the moment I approach the girl I will be thinking about sleeping with her today. Every time I go out, there is an opportunity to meet women, and have sex. There is a world of sex out there. It is everywhere. Women love to have sex. It is open and available to those who know what to look for and are skilled, bold and masculine enough to go and take it!

I am a caveman - The more primal I get the more I feel myself in tune with my core. I always think like a caveman, eat like a caveman, act like a caveman, fuck like a caveman.

I am a purely R-selected - I am the sex guy. When I meet with a girl only thing I think of is fast casual sex. My actions and intentions follow this. I don't care about her quality according to society's eyes but I care what kind of sexy thoughts she would make me think if she came to my bedroom naked.

I deserve to sleep with beautiful women - I really do deserve to sleep with beautiful women because I did sleep with many beautiful women.

I deserve to sleep with young women - Age difference is nothing if I am not presenting myself as the provider. I know that many girls liked me up to 15 years of age difference and I could sleep with several of them.

I am the best thing that can happen in her life - I have a great character, experience, culture, sexuality, enough money, good looks, good heart and great sex abilities. She really cannot find a better person than me to fuck who has everything overall. I won't be her provider anyway so I am enough for any women. I am important and valuable and I know that if she misses me it's because of her stupidity.

I am rich - I have enough money to satisfy all my desires. I am rich enough to enjoy a great life. Happiness is not found in seeking more, but in developing the capacity to enjoy less. I have simple needs and I have enough money to satisfy all these needs. I am getting richer every day. I am on my way to earn more than I need. All the money I am going to earn is already waiting for me.

I am financially free - Being rich would mean nothing to me if I were to be a CEO and would still wake up to go to work in the morning, get a salary and live in the commandment of the big boss. It is still a rat race. I earn my own money without being slave for anyone. If I want to do something, I do it, I don't get permission from anyone and I always have enough money for my needs. I am financially free to live the life I want to live.

I am capable of doing great things - I never underestimate the power of my mind. I may be poor or broke but from 5 years from now I never know what may happen. A business idea may pop up in my mind and I may act on it to build a great wealth. Anything can happen in this world so I should know that I are capable of doing great things.

My Visualisation Script

Below is my visualisation script. I visualise a part of my life as if I am living it. This can be a weekend you spend with a girl you love, buying yourself a new sports car and taking her from work or travelling abroad to see new places.

Your visualisation script has to be in line with your affirmations since you will listen affirmations at night and visualize through the day. The more detailed it is the better. The more sounds, colors and visuals the better. If you want to write everything in detail then write the points as I do and let your mind add the details.

In the example below when I write "Now we go to a bar holding hands on a rainy night." I visualise a dark street, umbrella, christmas lights, having fun talking, getting into bar. etc.

Weekend in Kiev

1. *I am in Kiev now with my Ukranian girlfriend. This is friday evening and we go to an Italian restaurant together.*
2. *She is beautiful and she has a great character. I enjoy being with her and we enjoy a great time together.*
3. *Now we're having a delicious meal in the restaurant, looking at the beauty of my girlfriend, I am thinking how I will fuck her today.*
4. *Now we go to a bar holding hands on a rainy night. I feel myself great.*
5. *We are in the bar now. We drink a little here, we listen to music. I love the sound. I love living.*
6. *Now we walk on the way home. We hold hands together. It's a lovely house in the city center.*
7. *We come home and start having sex like crazy.*
8. *We sleep hugging each other.*

9. *I wake up in the morning, do my work when she's asleep. I realize that have more than enough money. Customers are happy and my work sells great. I love what I do. I love my life.*

10. *My girlfriend wakes up. We kiss and have a great morning sex.*

11. *We now go out take a stroll through the city. We eat a great breakfast.*

12. *Now we are in the cinema. Eating popcorn.*

13. *We now go to a Japanese restaurant, we have sushi.*

14. *We now go to a techno club that plays electronic music. We dance.*

15. *We are at home now and we have sex like crazy.*

16. *I get up in the morning. I check my work and see that sales are great. I feel so grateful.*

17. *I go to the supermarket and get food to prepare a great breakfast at home. We eat together.*

18. *We go out to get food to prepare at home.*

19. *We're at home now. We're drinking wine and watching a movie.*

20. *Now we are having sex again. Every day I have great sex.*

21. *It's a Monday morning and I leave her to work and go to the gym.*

22. *I am in the gym now working like an animal.*

23. *I'm on my way back home to work on my business all week long. This week is going to be a great week.*

Record Your Script

Start with these steps to create your own affirmation and visualisation scripts with background music. I cannot provide you scripts because It has to be in your own voice .

1- Install a voice recorder app to your phone.
2 - Go to a quiet room to read your script
3- Read your script this way;
For the affirmations read every line slowly as possible 3 times. Leave 2 second in between the repetitions and 4 seconds between each line. For example if you reading "I am rich", read that slowly three times with 1 second intervals and pass on to "I am financially free" in 3 seconds.
I am a warrior (read 3 times)
I am imperfect (read 3 times)
I am rich (read 3 times)
I am financially free (read 3 times)
For the visualisation read every line slowly once and then pause for 30 seconds. For example read "Now we go to a bar holding hands on a rainy night." and pause 30 seconds (to make your mind fill the details when visualising) and then pass to "We are in the bar now".
4 - Download background music. Go to youtube, download this music as mp3; this music. https://www.youtube.com/watch?v=CreU9g302yU
5- Download audacity app to your computer and run the app.
6 -You will create the audio in this way;
For affirmation script import both the script mp3 and background mp3. The background music is 1 hour long. Your script may be 5 minutes. So you will duplicate the affirmation script 12 times and place them side by side. At the end there should be a 1 hour long voice record.

For the visualisation script you don't have to repeat it since you need it just for 15 minutes session. Consider your script one more time. Mine has 26 points. 4 seconds on average to read a point and 30 seconds to wait and its 15 minutes on average. Your script should be similar not to exceed 15 minutes.

7 -Export the audio and create an mp3 from that. Repeat 1 to 7 for both scripts.

8 -Upload the scripts to your phone.

Your Affirmations Script

I want you to listen to your script for the rest of your life when you are sleeping. Yes, you heard it right. Not 3 months not 6 months, for the rest of your life, every single day. In addition to that read the explanations of the affirmations every week.

Your script will eventually change according to your needs and desires but you should never ever drop your programming session. Just drop it once and eventually you will quit and you will surely return to your old programming. Do it every single day. It should be part of you.

You should listen to it every single day at night, like a religious person prays every single day. It's so practical and doesn't take time so it shouldn't be a problem. So get ready to commit doing it. If you continue doing it, in 3-6 months time you will start to run on autopilot from your program.

Your Visualisation Script

I want you to listen to your guided visualisation script once every day, preferably after your workout or 15 minutes after you wake up. Don't be afraid to visualise crazy things even though they are far away from your current situation. Visualise different parts from your new life and so it will be real. Create different visualisations for different things you want to live. I have 4 different visualisation scripts that are all about my affirmations in different situations. Key here is to do it everyday religiously.

Assignments

Approach 20 Women

Approach 20 women as I have written on day 1.

Write Your Daily Journal

Write your daily journal as I have written on day 1.

DAY 15 - OPENING | VIBE

Introduction to Opening

As you understand, we came up to technicals of "how to approach and seduce women" only in week 3. This is because if your mindset is wrong, technicals won't help you. I can very easily say that %90 in success with women is your mindset that comes from your beliefs (reptilian brain) and %10 is the technicals (middle and upper brain). From now on I will explain to you the exact technicals of opening and escalation while still building on your foundation of raw sexual desire. I will also include some "game" theory because it has its place and it will help you to speed up the process.

Importance of Vibe

All humans, but especially women, have the ability to pick up on "Vibe." It is the vibration you give out. As Nikola Tesla said, we all vibrate energy. It's the "state" I'm talking about. In flow state you give great vibe.

Have you ever seen someone who was so scared or angry, or happy, that they physically shook? High levels of emotion actually causes your body to vibrate, your hands to fidget, your face to twitch, your eyes to widen.

So say you approach a woman and she's having a great day. You on the other hand, are nervous, anxious, and scared. Your vibrations will not match. Your vibe of fear and self-consciousness will overpower her chill, happy vibe, and cause her to feel fear. She will tune into your frequency.

If you're feeling horny, confident, happy, relaxed, in control, and you approach a woman who is on the same frequency, you will harmonize. If she is feeling down, fearful, or anxious, and your positive vibe is stronger, she will be compelled to tune into your vibe.

We've all spoken to people who aren't really saying anything to turn us off, but there's just something about them that communicates an unhappiness. Maybe it's a deep insecurity that is preventing them from truly expressing themselves. You might say their vibe is just a bit off.

When starting out, the reason you may get blown out a lot when approaching women, is because your vibe will be far too serious. It's not necessarily a negative vibe, but it's not one that rescues a girl from her boring day to give you attention.

When you persevere, you will inevitably come across a really friendly, sexy girl who gives you a really positive response, which reminds you that you are actually a cool, high value guy. When this happens your manner towards approaching women get different. You will be more comfortable, have more fun, your vibe will change. You will be more confident and genuine.

Your vibe needs to communicate that you are a sexual and a playful person. Whether you start like that or you become that after warming up; no girl wants to unwrap it to find a bitter person full of hatred, anger and self-pity. They want to find a shiny ball of sexiness, fun and happiness.

How To Have a Great Vibe

Cultivate desire

I personally have suffered a lot from depression. The reason I was suffering was I wasn't solving the problems I had to solve in my life because I was afraid to lose what I already had. You can masturbate, take drugs, drink or intellectualize to hide your problems, but as long as you don't solve your life problems, they will always come up.

So after years of sitting on the couch and numbing myself, I realised that I had to get out and do something. Once I took the steps to solve my problems, even though I was suffering financially and emotionally, I started to feel better. Because I knew I was on the right track. And once I started the get out little results, I was no longer in depression. I started to become too busy getting better.

So if you've got shit going on in your life and if you don't do something to solve it, then it will just mess with every area of your life including women.

I recommend you to use pain, frustration and anger to your advantage and stay away from everything that numbs you (masturbation, drugs, alcohol, nicotine, caffeine, toxic people, tv, etc.). Pain, frustration and anger are vital feelings to change your life because you can use them to create desire. Pressure creates diamonds. Use them to get obsessed and use them to fuel your desire.

If you have bitterness towards money, then let it fuel your desire to get rich. If you don't like how you look, use that to push you going to gym and giving your all. If you feel frustrated that you are lonely, use that to meet with more women and find the woman you love. Recycle your pain and turn your pain into desire, action and greatness. There is only one thing that can change you. One thing. That thing is called "Action". When you have shit going on in your life, the worst thing you can do is to sit at home and do nothing. Remember Newton's law; an object at rest stays at rest and an object in motion stays in motion.

Visualise Success

Visualise yourself going out there today, smiling all the time, taking rejection after rejection, still smiling knowing that you will meet with your girl, then actually meeting with a hot girl. Visualise the once painful process as if it is something pleasurable and necessary for your success. Visualise how you finally meet with her. How you perfectly approach her. How you connect, how you touch her. Visualise how you take her to a coffee shop, then taking her to a bar and coming back home. Visualise fucking her in every detail. Forget about getting numbers, forget about dates, forget about relationships. I want you to see the possibility of fucking her today so you will give out the right sexual responses. This will automatically create your playful and sexy vibe.

Do Not Depend on Vibe

There will be days that you will feel down and nothing will help you. You must still go out and try those days and this is why you must never depend on your vibe (state). You cannot give yourself the excuse of not feeling well. Ultimately what you want is to meet and seduce the women you like anytime and anywhere. Best opportunities always come in unexpected situations. If you depend on your state for doing that, you will use it as an excuse not to take action.

Having said that, after you mass approach women, feeling of being in the zone is addictive because it fills you with the perfect vibe you can ever have even your life is failing. It spikes you up. So what I must recommend is to aim for getting the zone and when you are there use it to its maximum extent. However, never ever depend on it, never ever use not having in the zone as an excuse to not take action.

The ability to get into zone increases with practice. The more you go out meeting with women, the more you train yourself, the more you get used to managing your emotional state. Eventually, just through repeatedly going out, you will build up the ability to manage your emotions so that you don't talk yourself out of state.

Allocate Certain Time

Building your vibe to get into zone starts with allocating a specific time of your day to meeting with women. Ultimately you want to meet and seduce the women you like any time and anywhere but if you don't train consistently you won't be able to do that. If you say to yourself that you can do, you are talking out of your ego and you are risking your potential.

As I wrote before, see meeting women like going out to the gym. Doing 200 pounds bench press without a daily training is risking your injury. Meeting and seducing women is the same thing. If you don't go out and train consistently, you will eventually quit. By quitting I mean masturbating. By quitting I also mean settling with the girl you found. By quitting I mean when you see a hot girl you like in a cafe, finding reasons not to talk with her.

When you masturbate or when your girlfriend waits in your bed, of course you won't go out there and take the rejections. I've been there, I've done that. However, over time, not only you'll lose your ability to get into state, you'll find back your crippling approach anxiety. The more you lose your abilities, the more you won't go out so the more you will masturbate or get needy for her. These are totally unconscious patterns.

So I recommend you this. If you don't have any woman in your life, go out everyday for 2-3 hours until you find sex. Give yourself no way and no day out. If you found sex but not consistently or not with a girlfriend you like/love, then still go out 5 days a week for 1-2 hours. If you found a girlfriend you like/love then still go out 3 times a week for 1-2 hours to meet with women. I don't count going up to a hot girl you see on your way to work in the metro. I talk about the time you allocate to your training in a crowded place that you approach every 300 seconds.

See it as going to the gym. If you do this, you will always have an abundance of quality women in your life. You will also have the best relationships because you will never be needy. She will be afraid to lose you so she will give you the best sex and manners to keep you.

Assignments

Approach 20 Women
Approach 20 women as I have written on day 1.

Write Your Daily Journal
Write your daily journal as I have written on day 1.

DAY 16 - OPENING | TARGET SELECTION

Determine The Woman You Like

You cannot get every woman. Let's leave the availability issues such as her being married or having a boyfriend, many of them simply won't be into you or the way you present yourself. This is why the main rule of target selection is; <u>aim to pen those girls for whom you really feel attraction.</u>

Of course this is an aim and doesn't mean you should not go for a women you would sleep if she came to your room naked. You should. Especially when you are training you will go up to these women to keep you in state, but you must be a man who knows what he wants and recognises it when he sees it.

However, you can't fuck just any woman with a heartbeat. You should be able to quickly pick one out from the crowd and know why you chose her. That's why you absolutely must determine what type of women you like. When you do that you will feel like the selector and the she will think you chose her for a reason. When you see this type of woman, you know you're going to approach, the approach anxiety will almost diminish.

When you get clear about what you want, think of your dream girl. How do you want her to look like. How you want her to dress. How you want her to be. Write the list of qualities you want from a woman, and a list of qualities that will cause you to screen a woman out.

I like nerdy slavic women with colored hair such as red, pink, gray, blue. What girls do you like? This will predispose certain types of girls to liking you, and actually these girls will better fit to you naturally. At the end of the day most of your success will come from your niche. You should still expand your horizons and go after girls that are not in your niche but you shouldn't expect much from them.

There is also another factor that you should consider when you are meeting with women, especially during the daytime. Feminine girls who enjoy taking the submissive role will respond positively to your masculine push will be attracted to your approaches.

Masculine girls, who are generally attracted to monetary status, good looks and youth won't respond to you as much as the feminine girls. So always try to find feminine girls and don't disappoint yourself with the negative reactions of masculine ones. Use them as practice as they use men.

Focus on doing it

Don't focus too much on target selection in the beginning. You cannot only approach your dream girls, you will still have to keep the interval to be "fit" when you finally meet with her. The reason I say is you simply won't find enough of your dreams girls around. Even when you find, most of them will be taken. So always be R-selected and go for pretty much any girl you'd fuck if she comes to your room naked. When the available dream girl comes up, you will know.

Until then, get the work done. Focus on doing the task at hand rather than losing time selecting the best girl. When you are totally comfortable with whom you are and what you are doing, you will feel yourself great and you will select the right targets. Choosing your targets according to phase you are and in a manner congruent with your intentions should be your aim. Rejection, insults and bad behaviour should never affect you.

Target selection for training

Choose any girl you would fuck if she came to your bedroom naked. In this way not only will keep the interval alive but you will be ready for the girls you are interested. To maximise your effectiveness without losing time, approach these three kinds of girls.

First and foremost, approach the girls of exactly your type. These are your dream girls who have the characteristics you want. When you see her, you are approaching her and you are approaching her perfectly. You can't lose her.

Second, approach girls you would fuck if she came to your bedroom naked. She may be a very beautiful girl in society's eyes or she may be an average girl who you think is sexy. Put them all in the same category and approach to keep interval alive. Don't forget, you are looking for your dream girl, not this type of girl even though she may be beautiful.

Finally approach girls who project an approachable vibe. The girls who walk slowly and in a dreamy fashion. A tourist girl looking around trying to find where to go next. A sad girl who may have broken up with her boyfriend. They may not be the most beautiful girls but since they don't have anything else going on in the moment, they are likely to respond. These girls will give you the highest same day sex possiblity.

Target selection for daily life

When you are not training you should only go for the girls of exactly your type or the girls who make your blood bubble. Let's say you are in a public transport commuting to work and you see a girl you think really hot. Walk up to her, calmly and confidently, and tell her exactly what you like about her.

Don't really think she's hot? Don't bother approaching. The girls you meet in real life coincidences have much higher chances of being with you than the girl you met on the street or in bars. However, you will get the best results when you go up to them trained so you will come from an experienced and genuine place. For her, nothing is more sexy than meeting with the guy she likes spontaneously.

When you are in a bar or club you should select the girls who are already isolated however this doesn't mean you can't go up to groups. Remember that it's between you and her and act accordingly. She may buy a drink, go to the toilet or stand distant from her friends. Try to select these types of girls because it will be harder to isolate a girl who is already having fun with her friends. In these cases approach the group and tell them to excuse yourself for talking directly with her and do the same thing you do during daytime. Don't use the game theory of entertaining the group which is also way harder. Remember, it's between you and her.

Keep your eyes open and remember that every woman you come into contact with could equally be moaning with pleasure in your bed and behave accordingly towards her. Always check for your eye contact with women. A woman who looks at you as you pass by is very likely to respond. Remember; you are the guy who always hits on women regardless of his surroundings. Stop thinking in terms of day game, night game, tinder game or whatever. Your training on the street will give you the possibility to make this happen effortlessly. Because if you can do it on the street daily, you can do it anywhere, anytime. That's why it's so important to spare time of your day for the training.

Assignments

Approach 20 Women
Approach 20 women as I have written on day 1.

Write Your Daily Journal
Write your daily journal as I have written on day 1.

DAY 17 - OPENING | THE APPROACH

Remember Why You Approach Her

After you select your target, the biggest roadblock that can have between you and her is approach anxiety or what as I call it, approach avoidance. It starts with a tiny little thought of doubt and grows bigger and bigger to stop you from taking action - if you let it.

I call it avoidance because your choice of not risking hurting your ego and your avoidance of pain is what creates the physical or mental anxiety. It is no different than a guy who has a secure job not risking quitting it and opening his own company in a market where 9 out of 10 companies fail. This is actually an avoidance, anxiety is the byproduct.

Fear of rejection is the central reason for approach avoidance. To overcome it, you may choose to internalise the facts such as "everyone gets rejected" or "it's not about you" as other books write. However, as I said before, the fear comes from your lower brain. If you try to solve it by thinking, you are communicating with your upper or with your middle brain at most, but they will always lose to your lower reptilian brain. It is no different than trying to overcome the desire to sleep. Your willpower will run out eventually.

To solve a fear that comes from your lower brain, you must challenge it with another imperative from your lower brain such as the fear of losing money (survival) or by the pleasure of sexual desire (reproduction).

The fear of loss is always greater than the desire to gain pleasure. Think of a gun in your head challenge to approach 1000 girls today. You wouldn't do that to gain pleasure, but you would do it for sure. However, when you use the pleasure to go up to her, it makes her "vibe" sexual. When compared to going up to her by the incentive of fear, going up to her with the incentive of pleasure works better.

So, the solution to overcome approach avoidance is to communicate with your lower brain to use fear or your sexual desire to your advantage. I recommend sexual desire for the long run, however if you find yourself not taking action, use the fear.

This is why I created Bethabit. There are very socially anxious people out there and it's very hard for them to connect with their sexual nature from the get go. Bethabit makes them get used to meeting with women using fear, so their fear slowly but surely turns into an excitement and eventually they get connected with their sexual natures. That's the end result.

When you approach a woman you have to mean it, with real intent. Just before you approach her, you should remember the original reason why you approach her. You approach her because you want her sexually and you are hungry for sex. Men forget about this.

You are not doing it to find a friend, not to ask for directions, not to get her phone number, not to go on a date with her, not to impress your friends. You have to be doing it for your hunger that comes from your biological reproduction need. You approach her because you sexually want her now! Always remember this. When you see her, do you feel an instinctive desire for her? Hold onto that desire before you approach her.

If you hold on that desire, you will clear your mind of buzzing thoughts. Focus only on the attraction you are feeling in that moment. Don't try to rationalise anything. Don't intellectualise it. Don't think. Approach with the goal in your mind that you find her attractive and would love to fuck her today. Simple as that.

Don't hide this most basic fact from yourself, don't excuse it, and don't be embarrassed about it. It is perfectly natural. If you let your desire flow through you, and put your focus on her, it will filter through into your behavior. This is what turns her on at a primal level, creating the sexual tension. What you say has no importance after that. If it had importance, caveman wouldn't get laid for million years.

You want sex and in order to get sex there must be sexual tension. Solving approach anxiety is not enough. Somebody may put a gun to your head and push you to approach her and you will. Yes you will overcome the approach anxiety but the energy you give to her will be completely different than what I'm talking about. Use fear when necessary, but until you realize the power of your sexual energy.

Accept Approach Anxiety

I want to point out that even under the best conditions such as you loving your life and feeling horny; It is perfectly okay to be nervous. Approach anxiety is perfectly ok, avoidance is the problem. Courage is doing something despite the odds. That odd maybe a physical anxiety or a feeling that everybody looks at you, it's ok.

Avoidance creates the problem. You find yourself countless reasons not to approach and doesn't matter the reasons are right or wrong, the thinking part stops you. That's why another challenging fear or your sexual energy that comes from your primal instinct has to override the thinking part.

As long as you act authentically you can attract women being anxious, frustrated, miserable, angry or anything. The reason is because she is seeing that you are not afraid to show it, and it is real. Women respond better to authentic behaviour than a guy who doesn't put himself on the line and has no intent. Authenticity is way more important than your vibe.

If you think and place too much importance initially on her opinion of you and hence try to impress, this puts pressure on both of you immediately. If you approach a woman and are too caught up in how it will turn out, you will automatically start trying to "convince" her that you are a good bet.

On some level it is similar to approaching her like a beggar, except in this case you are asking her not for money but for her validation that you are an attractive man. This shows you are not secure in yourself and that you need the opinion of a woman to make you feel good about yourself. It is an emotional leeching and her instinctive response is to get away from you as quickly as possible.

Most guys who practice the "indirect game" start by asking for directions or opinions where they find themselves in a new comfort zone. Since they don't really put themselves on the line until they've received interest, this makes the interaction unauthentic. Remember the reason why you are approaching her. When asking for that stupid opinion opener, are you being authentic or not? Is there anything sexy about it?

Women are crying out for a real man to sweep them off their feet. They go around chasing their tails until a man grabs them and leads them off. They search for the right guy as much as you search for the right woman. Would you want your dream girl to approach you and ask you about bullshit?

Successful intimacy is the highest priority in every woman's life and thus any time she meets a potential, she will make the time to find out. Your direct sexual intent proves that you are a man, not a mouse.

Don't worry about "she looks busy" or "I'm interfering with her day". She wants you to interfere. The whole act of being a man is to penetrate her day, her mind, her body. She's always on your side, hoping you are that guy she's been waiting for all this time.

This is actually the main reason why women reject guys. Most of the time they reject a guy because of his lack of intent. She cannot take you seriously as a man because you do not represent a sexual threat. Thus she cannot entertain the notion of sleeping with you.

Usually due to a combination of bad posture and body language, a quiet manner, and a quiet or trembling voice, indirect stupid question or half assed direct intent make this happen. These characteristics signal the very opposite of masculinity. She doesn't see the intent and authenticity so she rejects you.

How to overcome this problem? <u>Approach her with full fucking sexual intent</u>. Make her remember you. How do you do that? <u>By training daily to get in tune with your vulnerability.</u>

Have a Clear Sexual Intent

Your sexual intent is a thick bandwidth of sexual energy which quietens everything else. It quietens the negative self-talk and the voices in your head that inhibit your ability to approach.

The key to a good approach is your sexual intent. That's what really stops her. Your sexual intent comes from your clear un-ashamed desire for her without giving any fucks if someone looks or if she rejects.

It presents itself in everything you do, such as your eye contact, voice, body language and look. Once you combine it with a strong stop to kill her momentum, she will give her full attention to you.

Let's assume you are on the street because most of the time you will be doing street stops. So you've seen the girl walking down the street and you liked her.

Look at her body and try to get aroused by her. Once you realize that you want her, try to find a playful archetype on how looks like. Your playful interpretation of who she is and how she makes you feel sexually will create your opener. You will be sexual but playful enough, not to scare her. I'll explain about the playful archetype in the lesson about opener tomorrow.

Don't worry too much about forming specific words for the opener. Let her walk past you, turn back right away and start to walk after her. You shouldn't be stalking her more than 30 seconds since stalking is rude, but you should make sure she is alone.

Give around 30 seconds to check if she is alone and make your-self aroused looking at her ass and hair. Imagine what you'll do to her ass once she's naked on your bed. Image your dick getting into that ass while holding her hair. Image spanking that that ass and shooting your load on that ass.

Get aroused like a hungry tiger seeing the gazelle and dwell on that feeling to forget if she is too rich, too young, is someone is looking or whatever life problem you have. Then immediately start jogging after her with a cheeky smile.

Now, when you are running up to her imagine a circle with 2 meter radius where the girl is in the center. Almost like a compass, while always keeping 2 meters radius, you have to pass through her left or right and stop 2 meters straight in front of her, on a 90 degree angle. Just like compass turns from 180 degrees to 90 degrees, from east to north while still keeping the 2 meter radius.

As you are running around the circle, when you get to 135 degrees, start making eye contact with her and lock your eyes. Until 90 degrees, never lose eye contact. You will stop her mainly by your eyes completely locked at her and two of your hand palms facing down as if you are telling her "calm down".

Following the 2 meters radius while making a turn, your eye contact and your cheeky smile is the key here. Because if you jog past her too close on a 180 angle, she may think that you'll steal her purse. If you stop her too close on the 90 degree angle, then she may be afraid that someone is attacking her. If you don't keep the eye contact, there won't be sexual tension and she'll think you are a salesman. And if you don't have a cheeky smile it won't tell her that you're doing something friendly.

It's little technically demanding as the opener and you won't do it perfectly most of the time but that's not a problem as long as you are authentic and sexually aroused. At the start you may misjudge distances and she may end up walking straight into you. That's why keeping the 2 meter radius of the circle and having the cheeky smile when you start running is important.

Believe She Wants You

No-one likes being persuaded of anything. Who likes a sales call? Everyone wants to continue believing whatever they want to believe, unless they are open-minded to the idea that they might be wrong. If you don't want to buy a certain product, you will not stand for a salesman trying to persuade you to buy it.

The most common type of rejection you'll get approaching girls directly on the street is caused by the reaction where she thinks you are some kind of salesman. This happens in other situations too. When you approach her in a shopping centre she may think you are a store clerk or in a bar, she may think you are a promoter.

Having the belief that you are bothering the girl and taking up her precious time causes this. This comes from your entitlement to her. The problem with believing you're bothering her is that it is communicated in your body language and voice, and how you react to her.

You will probably not stop her with any conviction, and probably talk quite softly. If you are running in front, you will not get completely in front, but leave enough space for her to easy walk past. She can sense this because women have maybe 10 times more intuition than men. When this happens you have almost no chance. Game over.

If you think you're bothering her, what category of people, based on her past experience, is she going to put you in? Who in the past has approached her and thought they were bothering her? salesmen, charity people and beggars! All of them know that everyone they approach does not want to talk to them and it's communicated by their gestures and sounds.

So what is the solution for this? First, you have to get aroused by her to say "fuck all the reasons, I am going to get her no matter what". You must have a clear sexual intent. Then you have to feel entitled. You have to believe in your gut that you are the best thing that happened to her.

As I repeat over and over again, women want you. They want to talk to you. Their life purpose is to find "the man". Believe that you are valuable and they want you. They instinctively always and always look for valuable men even if they are engaged. They definitely don't want to be sold something, but they definitely do want to hear a compliment from a high value man and feel his sexual energy.

Assume Rapport

When you see a woman you want to approach go up to her as if you've already been on a date with her. Assume that she knows you. Believe in it. Assume rapport. Assume success. Assume that you will have sex together. This is not a tactic, it's the law of attraction.

Remember a day when you were really tired. All of a sudden people around you started yawning too. Remember the other day that you were really happy and people around you will start to be happy. This happens because we are wired to mirror the energy of the room, mirror the other person. Remember; she feels what you feel.

So if you feel in your gut that it's your right to go talk with that girl, it's your right to kiss her, then she is going to buy into it. She will feel as if she has already known you.

You can exercise assuming rapport by making statements to her just after you meet with her. For example, if she has an amazing body and when you look at her you think she is a dancer, go and tell her "so how long have you been dancing". Talk with her as if you already know that she is dancing.

Kill Her Momentum

A girl when walking down the street has both mental and physical momentum. Her physical momentum is the fact that her body is physically moving in a certain direction. Her mental momentum is the thing she thinks at the time being.

You can't have a conversation with her when you're stood still but she never physically stops. Her mental momentum is not as obvious, but it's still just as important. In her mind, before you stop her she is thinking about where she's going. While she's still thinking, "I'm on my way to the grocery store," she still has mental momentum.

You have to engage her fully in conversation to rid her brain of this thought. Until this is done you can't hook her into a conversation in which she is fully present mentally. That's why getting in front of a girl and stopping her boldly, keeping eye contact and cheeky smile rather than coming in from the side is much more likely to kill her momentum both mentally and physically.

The same applies to a nightclub or a bar. If a girl is dancing, you should first stop her moving to communicate with her. You may better wait for her to return back from dance floor. If she is in the bar talking with her friends, you have to excuse yourself from the group for just talking with her to get her full attention.

In the street I don't think there's anything that will kill her momentum as quickly as getting right in front of her, and shamelessly blocking her path and looking at her eye to eye with a cheeky smile.

It's also very high value. It sub-communicates that you're sure of yourself and what you want is the most important thing, more important than her getting to where she is going or if somebody else is looking.

Guys who want to know how to approach girls in the day-time are often afraid they're just going to "bother" or "annoy" women or they will seem weird. They stop the girl from the side like a beggar.

Look. It's only weird if you make it weird. When you walk up to a girl with a feeling of "this is wrong, I shouldn't be doing this" it's that feeling that creates the "weird" vibe.

Get rid of that feeling using your sexual energy and both you and the girl will be able to relax and enjoy meeting one an-other. Most women would love to meet a guy during the day. It makes a better story than meeting someone at a bar and shakes up the monotony of a woman's day-to-day routine.

You must feel in your gut that it is perfectly normal to stop a girl on the street and talk to her. If you fully expect her to stay and talk, she will stay and talk. This is her chance to meet you, the best thing that happened to her, this is her chance to find successful intimacy with a bold confident man like you are.

However, all the girls have a fight or flight response and in-stinctively their answer is almost always will be flight when you approach.

That's why it is extremely important to get the first few sec-onds right. The primary way to do this is to mix your sexual energy with playfulness. When you are aroused you may get too serious, however you cannot be too serious because it will scare her and you won't be really bringing any positive energy to make the interaction stick.

That's why you have to dilute your sexual intent with some playfulness. In the first few moments you should put all your sexual energy to her in a not threatening way. Just a cheeky grin will do that for you. By entering with direct sexual intent and a cheeky grin, you immediately put the girl at rest while your commanding presence and sexual energy stops her on her feet locked.

Make sure you don't explode into her reality, but gently ease yourself there. When you stop her by running in front of her, glide past her and then smoothly stop her. As I said, imagining a 2 meter radius circle and following the circle like a compass will help you a lot.

Imagine that she became your girlfriend and you are going to fuck her for the 10th time. You are sitting with her on the bed after a Saturday dinner. You know you're going to fuck her very soon. How would you look at her? How would you talk with her?

That's the exact energy I'm talking about. You almost erected dick makes her feel how hot horny you are. You eyes locked to her eyes unashamedly telling her that you are going to fuck her hard today. Your speak slowly and your voice tone is re-laxed and deep conveying that she is yours. All your moves are relaxed and gentle, you don't take things fast. You have a cheeky grin on your face but not a serious glare, telling her you are ready to play.

Complete sexual intent mixed with playfulness. Never forget that what you do is intensely sexual and a bit amusing because you are giving a sexual come on to a random girl. You may be standing on a busy street where people rush home from work, but the substance of the communication between you and her is on the sexual plane.

Think of a "love bubble" that encapsulates you and her as Da-ygame guys say. You don't hear the crowd, you don't see what's outside. At that moment there is only you and her in that moment and at any moment you may take her to your house. That's where you find your sexual intent mixed with playfulness.

When In Doubt Approach Anyway

There are always cases when you can't immediately tell if the girl is attractive to you. She passed too fast, she turned around, she wears a hat, you couldn't fully see her face, she has an oversized pair of sunglasses, she looks nice from behind but she might be a ugly face, etc.

The answer is who cares if you liked that ass? Go anyway because you'll never ever going to know. As a rule of thumb; <u>when in doubt, approach anyway</u>. Because you will never know. You really won't know just by looking at her face or dress.

One day when I got out of the subway, I saw a great ass and couldn't stop myself but approached her without seeing her face. She didn't have a remarkable face but I ended up fucking that ass and loved it.

Another day I saw a hot young girl with Louis Vuitton handbag and thought she was the daughter of a rich guy who I can never get. I approached anyway and found out that she is just an ordinary store clerk with a fake handbag and lots of makeup.

Some other day I saw a sloppy dressed cute girl and thought she was a drug addict. I found out that she is a nationally known actress from a wealthy family who just divorced and having a bad day because of it. You will never know. When in doubt approach anyway and eject if necessary, there is nothing to lose. You are going up to her and telling "take it or leave it". That's all.

Approach Like a Machine

Approach like a machine using intervals. Every successful person has a system. A money (or whatever) making machine. Use a standard system to generate "leads". I wrote you how you should train using intervals of 300 seconds. Use it. Approach massively. I would always stick to massive amounts of approaches than walking around like a gay looking for my dream girls because they usually come up in very unexpected circumstances.

Assignments

Approach 20 Women

Approach 20 women as I have written on day 1.

Write Your Daily Journal

Write your daily journal as I have written on day 1.

DAY 18 - OPENING | OPENER

Make Opener Specific To Her

You may think that once you've stopped her on the street, what then? Well, don't think because your words are not getting the girl.

You are speaking to her with the language that got caveman laid before spoken language evolved. The words are just the things that fill the space. You attract the girl with your subcommunications that are defined by your sexual vibe. Words are not meaningless, but they are not the engine driving the seduction.

Consider your words as adding structure to move things along. Once your subcommunications are right, you can still attract the girl even both you don't speak the same language. You can open her with any opener however it's best to make the opener specific to how that girl makes you feel. What I mean is, you are not doing openers that are canned.

If you are opening girls with openers that you read on the internet then you are just limiting your success. When you use prepared openers, you are shutting down the connection between what you feel and what you say with your words and she knows you are saying the sort of things you'd tell any girl.

Another fact is that it doesn't matter where you deliver the opener. It may be in a street, in a bus stop, a coffee shop, a bar or club. It doesn't matter because you are being direct and authentic, you are not gaming, you are saying something to start the conversation, that's all.

Opening does not get you laid. But when done correctly an opener will not only get you into a conversation, it will also build attraction and comfort from the start.

So let's say you stopped the girl and got her full attention and displayed positive masculine traits with your sexual energy , eye contact, voice and body language. Now what to say to her?

Now you let her know why you are talking to her. Let her know why you chose her and not any other girl. You start by saying "Hi" and continue with "I just have to say something" to get her attention and to be socially normal. Then you give her reason why you are talking with her saying "I was just over there when I saw you walk past".

Have a little pause and then and continue with "I loved how you look with this yellow summer dress you are wearing". Then you finalise the opener with "you look like those beautiful princesses from Disney cartoons" tease.

Women love a genuine compliment and in this way you state your romantic interest to her. The comical tease here tells her that "this is funny" and "this is playful". Princess from disney cartoons, eskimo from north pole or sweet witch with a broom.

When your direct sexual intent mixes with being playful, this immediately gets her attention and tells her that interaction with you is going to be enjoyable. After delivering the tease, don't speak Just stand looking at her with a playful smile and strong look to her eyes.

Your subcommunication is telling her "OK, I've said my piece. Now it's your turn". Let the silence hang in the air until she starts talking.

If she sees your genuine intent and feels your sexual energy, she will accept the compliment. Social etiquette requires it too.

So now not only have you added some value with your compliment and forced her through social etiquette to respond, but the gentle tease has given her something to respond.

If she responds and laughs then you should continue working on the tease. For example you can continue making an assumption statement about the tease such as "so you like to watch Disney cartoons...". She'll either answer with a positive response so conversation will flow naturally.

Now she is in a conversation with a stranger about Disney cartoons. You don't ask her what she does for a living right away. You don't ask where she is from or where she lives. It's just a casual but fun and sexual conversation with a guy on the street.

Tease is the key here. It doesn't matter if it sounds a bit stupid. You are diluting your sexuality with the playfulness you have so she won't be scared but feel your sexual energy. Your tease doesn't have to be logical. It just have to be playful.

If she doesn't get the tease or misinterpret it as an insult, you have to soften your approach without getting nervous. Just tell her it was meant as a tease, and then continue.

Specific Opener Examples

Here are some examples you can use. It doesn't matter where you use them. You can use them in a club or street. Only in a club or bar if she is with her friends, just excuse yourself to the group for talking with her.

At the end of the day what is important is how you form the opener according to how she makes you feel. You can still meet and seduce any girl with the opener "hi" as long as your energy is right and your energies match.

In general you first get her attention to say something by "Excuse me..I just have to say you something". Then you give a compliment such as "You look nice" or "I love the way you look". Then you continue with what you liked or noticed about her such as "what I noticed about you is how tall and blonde you are".

Then you introduce a comical tease of her playful archetype such as "you look like a viking just came by her ship to invade the city". Then you continue with a story about the archetype such as "so where is your viking hat and your wild friends, I can't see any of that, are you lost?". In this way you bridge your opener into real conversation.

Please don't use these examples as canned openers. Every opener has to be specific to how that girl makes you feel. These are just examples, actually real life talks from my experiences. Always improvise because you are an authentic man not a pickup artist. Especially when you are in the zone these talks will come automatically.

Girl with a french hat

You: Hi. I just have to say you something

Her: ok

You: I was just over there when I saw you walk past...I loved how beautiful you look..and I loved your french hat...I guess you were working on your latest piece of postmodern art and just came down to buy some coffee..

Her: (Smiles) no I actually just wear that hat. I'm not an artist.

You: I see...you have an aura of an artist though...you must be doing something artistic in your free time.

Her: I like to dance actually.

You:Oh, there you are...so you do salsa..

Girl with big boots during daytime

You: Hi. I just have to say you something

Her: ok

You: I was just over there when I saw you walk past...I loved how beautiful you look with your big stylish boots...you look like you were riding a horse and just got out of the horse.

Her: Oh, thank you. No I'm wasn't riding a horse (she smiles).

You: From the jacket and boots you wear..you look like a girl who likes riding horses or walking in nature..

Her: Yeah..I like walking in nature.

You: I like that too..so I guess you like walking in the forest to collect mushrooms...

Short girl with cute face during daytime

You: Hi. I just have to say you something

Her: You can.

You: I was just over there when I saw you walk past and I loved how you looked beautiful when you walked that fast...you were walking near the courthouse I guess you will get a divorce

Her: Thank you(she smiles)..actually I'm going for a meeting

You: So you are business woman who just divorced..

Girl with long hair during daytime

You:Hi. I just have to say you something

Her: ok

You:I was just over there when I saw you walk past and I loved how long your hair is...you look like Rapunzel
Her: Thank you.
You: so I hope the witch didn't see you when you run away from your tower
Her: No she didn't (smiles)
Me. so I guess you are shopping for your long hair..

Girl with messy hair during daytime

You:Hi. I just have to say you something
Her: ok
You: I was just over there when I saw you walk past and I loved how sophisticated your hair looks...you look like Tarzan's girlfriend Jane.
Her: Is that a compliment? (smiles)
You: yeah you look wild with your hair and dress..It's so sexy..I like it
Her: Thank you
Me. so where is the next place you are jumping?..I know a coffee shop over there that I can take you.

Girl with full black dress during daytime

You: Hi. I just have to say you something
Her: ok
You: I was just over there when I saw you walk past and I noticed your black dress...you look like a cute witch
Her: thank you(smiles)
You: so I guess you are outside to collect some frogs from your latest spell..
Her: No I don't
You: Are you going to do it with black cats this time? How does that work?
Her: No I don't
You: But I'm just trying to find out there your spell comes from..I'm just dazzled as you see.

Girl with tattoos all over her arm during daytime

You:Hi. I just have to say you something

Her: ok

You: I was just over there when I saw you walk past and I noticed your tattoos and how great you look with them...you look like you are a soloist in a rock band.

Her: thank you(smiles)

You: so I guess you just finished your concert, I would love to listen to how you play...

Girl with big furry coat during daytime

You: Hi. I just have to say you something

Her: ok

You:I was just over there when I saw you walk past and I noticed you..with your nice big furry coat you look like a cute beautiful eskimo.

Her: thank you(smiles)

You: so I think you are going to buy some food to eat in your igloo..

Girl with white coat during daytime

You:Hi. I just have to say you something

Her: ok

You:I was just over there when I saw you walk past and I thought you look nice

Her: thank you

You: what I noticed about you is your big white coat..you look like a snowman from north pole.

Her: oh really.

You: Yeah, did you just came from north pole?

Girl with leather jacket during daytime

You:Hi. I just have to say you something

Her: ok

You:I was just over there when I saw you walk past and I thought you look nice

Her: thank you

You: what I noticed about you is your leather jacket..you look like a member of a biker gang.

Her: oh no.

You: Well, you look quite adventurous...I bet you got tatoos.

Girl with red dress during daytime

You: Excuse me. I just have to say you something.

Her: ok

You: I was just over there when I saw you walk past and I thought you look nice

Her: thank you

You: what I noticed about you is the red dress you're wear-ing..you look like little red riding hood.

Her: oh really.

You: Well, I can't see your bread crumbles around, where are they?

Girl with yellow dress during daytime

You: Excuse me. I just have to say you something.

Her: ok

You: I was just over there when I saw you walk past and I thought you look nice

Her: thank you

You: what I noticed about you is the yellow dress you're wear-ing..you look like a princess from disney movies

Her: oh really.

You: Yeah, it's been a long time since I watched a disney ani-mation..what's your favorite one?.

Girl with tattoos and friends in a bar

You: Hi...I'm John..I hope you are having a great night(look at the group)

Them: Yeah, thank you.

You: I saw your friend over there(look at the girl you like) and I couldn't stop myself coming here and saying hi to her..she looks so beautiful(look at her).

Her: thank you.

You: Would you excuse me if I only talk with her? (look at the group)

Them: why not.

You: Hi..I love the Egyptian symbols in your tattoos...I think you are an egyptian goddess who happen to visit San Francisco (let the group hear what you say).

Her: Yeah I do(smiles).

You: So you've been to Egypt and made your tattoos in there...

Leggy girl buying drink alone in a bar

You: Can you make some room so I can get some drinks for my friends? This bar is crazy (hold her arm)

Her: Yeah of course.

You: Thank you. I like how you look. It's like you are coming here from a salsa class having danced with some amateurs.

Her: why do you say that?

You: Because I can't dance but your hips, your long legs and your incredible ass tells me that you can dance.

Girl with long eyelashes dancing in a club

You: Hi, can I tell you something

Her: Yeah

You: I was just over there when I saw you dancing and I thought you look nice

Her: thank you

You: what I noticed about you is your innocent but potentially dangerous look..your long eyelashes have something to do with that..you look like a character in a Japanese anime I love.

Her: oh really.

You: Yeah, you look like Mikasa in Attack of Titans..she was so innocent but used to cut big giants without mercy..so I guess you hide some great ability behind your innocence.

Assignments

Approach 20 Women
Approach 20 women as I have written on day 1.

Write Your Daily Journal
Write your daily journal as I have written on day 1.

DAY 19 - OPENING | FLIRTING

Project Your Sexual Energy

After you deliver the opener you have to project your sexual energy to her. Many men go wrong after the opener because they get caught in boring or fun conversations that go no-where because they don't know how to create sexual tension.

To avoid this, you need to transition from social to sexual. You have to always remember your purpose for the inter-action which is sex. Continue having a clear sexual intent as you did have before approaching her. Look at her, appreciate her, look at her legs and ass and breasts and appreciate her as a feminine creature.

Look at her beauty. Do whatever it takes but try to capture that sexual feeling within yourself. Just that. Don't let any-thing else intrude such as "I'm not good enough," "I'm ner-vous," or "I'm scared." Just the feeling of lust and honest appre-ciation should be there. Focus on that feeling. You can create sexual tension by thinking of her in a sexual way and appreci-ating her beauty.

Keep holding a strong sexualised eye contact with her. As you're talking to her, you should aim to keep eye contact as long as possible but not in a threatening way. Try and hold her eyes and smile at appropriate points. Don't stare!

The beauty of the girl, her scent, the way she moves, the feel-ing in your cock and balls, the shifting of the cells within your body...let that bring you into the moment. When you're look-ing at her, drank her in and really imagine the naughty things you will do to her. She will feel your energy and that's what she longs for. You have to give a woman what she wants, which is sexual tension.

She is going through her daily life, probably in her own kind of boring job, and then in you roll and you start. When you mix it with having fun it is extremely entertaining for her.

Project Your Playfulness

The way to get the most out of the open and escalate model is to bring in lots of fun and playfulness in the interaction with her while keeping the sexual tension. It also shows that you are not affected by her beauty, unattainability, or her appearance of high social value. I'm not talking about creating a comedy show or being a clown.

Have you ever noticed that you can tell a funny story and make them laugh, if you yourself are having fun and you are in the present moment? Conversely, if you are feeling tired, anxious or hoping for a good response when you tell the exact same story no one laughs?

So in order to have fun, you have to retain a positive outlook and feel happy and content with yourself. Then you will realise what's funny or quirky in the present moment and tell that without caring about any response.

You won't really find things amusing if you're in a negative frame of mind. It won't happen if you think whether it will go well or whether it will impress her. Having fun implies her that you are safe in your own skin and you are living in the present moment. Why would you not care about the outcome?

Because you are enjoying the moment and you are confident enough to say something you find funny to others, without worrying if they will like it. Why would you not care if they like it or not? Because you are socially confident, with high self-esteem and social awareness, and hence have no worries about what others think.

It should be childlike. A child has not yet learned to be quiet, and self-aware. A child lives in the present moment and is not constrained by "the rules". A child is having fun and he is playful. Child wants that toy.

Especially during the daytime, the girl has a very short initial attraction phase because she is usually occupied with her life and not considering herself open to meeting the way girls in nightclubs are. Thus <u>it is extremely important to get the first few seconds right with an overload of attraction</u>. The primary way to do this is to inject your sexual vibe to her and have fun. Seriousness just kills your vibe.

What you do is very self amusing. You are going up to a random girl on the street and trying to fuck her. If you're not having a bit of fun then there's something wrong with you. Girls want to have fun.

Flirt With Her First

The biggest mistake guys do after delivering an opener is going straight to the comfort without flirting with the girl. They usually start telling about themselves or try to find out about her by asking personal questions such as:" what do you do?" or "where are you from?".

Problem with that is the girl doesn't know you yet. She won't be engaging with you properly. You just stopped her and she will be like "Who are you" or "why should I tell you about who I am". By flirting with her first; you get her emotions going and you get her slightly aroused. So when you do get to the comfort phase she will be interested in you and she will be willing to share about who she is with you.

For a girl to come to a date with you she has to feel attracted to you and then she has to feel comfortable to you. Your sexual energy creates the physical attraction but you have to dilute it with playfulness. Do that it by flirting with her first.

Teasing

Teasing is a way of flirting that sets you apart from the nice guys who are trying to get stuff by being nice. Nice guys only give girl compliments but they don't tease her because they are afraid that she will misunderstand teasing.

When you tease the girl you show her that you are not one of those nice guys, you are having fun and you are using her for your own amusement. When you are not teasing her, it means there is a disconnect between you and her.

Remember a time when you were teasing somebody. Most probably he was your best friend or she was your girlfriend. If you transplant the symbolism of this to your interaction with new girls then you're on to a winner.

The most crucial aspect of teasing is that it creates a child like atmosphere and you cannot get a better rapport and connection with her than a child like in-the-moment vibe. Because it is the time that you were yourself. So at least going for teasing, not backing away from teasing, not fearing, creates the connection with her.

When you are teasing the girl always smile. However you should not have a cheesy smile, it should be a cheeky smile. A subtle smile communicates her that what you do is playful. Teasing is supposed to be fun and it shouldn't insult the girl. You cannot tell her something like "You're pretty awful at thinking logically, aren't you? Maybe you should stick to emotions". This will hurt her.

A great frame you can use is a dad teasing his little daughter. Father teases his little daughter but he doesn't want to hurt her or make her upset. That's what you want to be doing.

When you are teasing her you should avoid commenting on sensitive topics. These include physical features, style and fashion, intelligence, social skills, family, or anything like that. You cannot tell her that she is fat, short or unfashionable. What you can tease her should be more about her funny character traits such as her laugh, her seriousness or naughtiness.

Your teases also has to be critique-free. If you don't like how a girl does something, that's ok but don't tease her about it. If you want to talk about it, tell it seriously. For example rather than teasing her with "oh, do you listen pop music just like school girls?". Tell her "yeah..I used to like pop but when I discovered electronic music I never listened to pop again".

It's best to tell teases that include yourself. Don't let a girl get cast into the tease alone. You go with her. For example, if she doesn't understand something don't tell her "I hope you won't make me explain this ten times". Tell her "hey, are you just trying to confuse me and throw me off the trail right?".

When you're teasing a girl the right way, you'll know it. Her attraction will tell you your teasing is good and her closeness tells you are doing it right. Below are some examples;

I Don't Believe You Teases

One way of teasing is whenever she says something or makes a comment, tell something playfully contrary to her. Tell her "I don't believe you" and make a playful comment about it. For example;

Her: I am a doctor
You: I don't believe you. You look like an artist, you are pretending to be like a doctor.

Her: I am from Italy.
You: I don't believe you. Are you sure you are from Italy? Because you look like a cute Russian girl.

Playful Archetype Teases

Another way to tease the girl is compare her with an archetype while stating your romantic interest. That's why it's best to create this archetype before you approach her and tell her in the opener so you can build on it as tease

You: I like your pretty face, when you smile you look like a fluffy tailed squirrel that has nuts inside her mouth...I want to feed you with nuts to see how beautiful your smile is.

You: I like the way you walk, it's so sexy, you look like beautiful cat looking around to catch her next prey.

You: I like how tall you are, you long legs gets all my attention, you look like a cute giraffe.

You: you look like that cartoon character...Heidi, remember her?

You: you look like my grandma coming home from bazaar to feed the kids...you are so cute.

You: you look like a rock girl with your leather jackets and boots. Are you playing in a band?

You: you look like a doctor in your long plain white dress. Are you going to your hospital?

You: hey I like your dress. You look like a hippie, I guess you've been smoking weed in the park.

You: hey you look like an artist. I imagine you've been doing some wild painting.

Embarrassing Trait Teases

You can also find her embarrassing personal trait and tell her without insulting her. You can also playfully tie that as the reason why you cannot be together. Try not to be too personal.

You: Don't look at me like that, I'm not a piece of meat!

You: I like that you're always laughing, I'm officially calling you giggles

You: hey..are you always this serious?..I'm thinking of discussing politics with you

Challenging

Far too many guys are all too happy with "please love me" vibe. Far many guys are too agreeable with the girl. You have to display that you are standing in your own ground. By getting into a challenge with her, you are displaying her what you believe in regardless of what anybody else including her thinks.

For example; you may like playing warcraft and she may tell that only nerdy guys play that game. You should never agree with her but challenge her "why do you think so, it's actually the most popular game in the world..do you think playing videos games makes a person nerd? ". You are not arguing with her, but you are standing in your ground.

Another example can be that you like modern art and she says modern art is not interesting she thinks classic art is better. In this case you may start talking about why modern art is different and how it actually created to overcome the limits of classic art. Idea is again is to stand your own ground.

Here are some examples I can give you;

Her: I think New York is the best place to live
You: I don't know, New York is too expensive. I wouldn't spend my hard earned dollars on renting a house in New York. Do you?

Her: I don't like techno music, it's too noisy
You: Well, why do you say that? those noises are called art. In the same way that classical music does actually, except classical is not danceable and precise as techno.

Her: I don't like cats, they are not loyal.

You: Why do you say that? Cats are free and loyal enough as long as you keep your borders and care about them.

Role Playing

Role playing is creating a fantasy situation where you and the girl are different archetypes such as different animals, characters or occupations. You can be a doctor and the patient, cat and dog or batman and the cat girl. When you introduce role playing into the conversation it makes really playful and subtly sexual.

There are two ways to start a role play. First can be about her physical appearance, second can be her character trait. For example, if she is wearing green/brown clothes like a hunter, you can make her the hunter and yourself the bear. If she is lazy or clumsy, you can make her a student and yourself her teacher.

Always make the role play characters specific to the girl. You cannot tell every girl who wears black a sweet witch. Tell it if you really think she looks like a witch.

Unlike sexual roleplay you won't be describing her a situation where you are having sex but you may want to subtly imply about sex. You may talk about situations where you are catching her or getting her to surrender to subtly imply about sex. For example, she may be a small animal and you may be a predator.

These are some examples;

You: you look like a bear hunter with this green barbour jacket. You know, my friends used to tell me bear.
Her: oh..really.
You:Yeah, when you are in the forest I can run over to you and hug you with my claws. You won't kill me right?

You: Your black dress and the way you walk on the street is

like you are a cute witch collecting frogs for her latest spell.
Her: oh maybe I am a witch.
You: So the way you look at me, I guess I am the frog you are looking for.

You: if you were to be an animal what would you be?
Her: a chipmunk. How about you?
You: I would be an eagle. And I would chase down on you, jump on you and catch you like this (hug her)

Assignments

Approach 20 Women
Approach 20 women as I have written on day 1.

Write Your Daily Journal
Write your daily journal as I have written on day 1.

DAY 20 - OPENING
| COMFORT

Make Assumptions

You are not playing character. You are not a pickup artist running routines. You know that your subcommunications are what actually gets the girl.

So you flirted with the girl and now you are not just a random guy who stopped her on the street or approached in a club. You are sexual and playful and you see she puts some input in the conversation and stays.

This is the time you should get to know each other. You already flirted with her and you see there is an attraction going because she stays. What is important in this point is to keep the conversation going. Make her know that you are a normal guy, get to know her, tell about yourself. Most important, keep the conversation going.

To keep the conversation going never forget the fundamental rule. "Make a statement about the last thing she said no matter what it is!".

It's only through making statements that you can demonstrate your personality, your character and thus your value as a man. You aren't going to demonstrate anything by just asking her a series of questions. Questions will sound like a job interview for her.

The simplest way to turn all your questions into statements is by making assumptions about her. Think of 'cold reading', except it doesn't matter too much if you're accurate. The cool thing about making an assumption about someone is that if you get it wrong, she will feel compelled to correct you.

If you get it right, she will feel compelled to tell you so. Either way, you're prompting an answer out of her, but by making a value giving statement – rather than a value taking question. By making assumptions you will able to talk, and keep talking and actually never run out of things to say ever again, because you can just make a statement about the last thing she said.

Rather than asking "What are you doing?" tell her "When I first saw you, the first things I noticed were your classy-looking suit, your perfect make-up. I think you're a business woman."

Rather than asking "Where are you from" tell her "What I noticed about you was the dark hair, the feminine way of dressing and how skinny you are. I think you're from China."

Rather than asking "What kind of job do you do?" tell her "What I noticed about you was the warm furry jacket, and the tight jeans. I think you work on a farm."

Conversational Follow-ups

When making a statement you should load it with a couple of nouns or emotions that act as conversational follow ups she can follow. When she makes a statement you should look for the conversational follow up she has given you.

For example when she introduces herself and tells you she is from Ukraine, the follow up here is Ukraine. You can make assumptions such as the things you love about Ukraine, your travel to Ukraine, Ukrainian food you ate or so on.

If she tells you that she is a student who works a lot now, you can follow up on "working a lot" and "student" by asking her which course makes her study that hard.

The same thing applies to you. If you are talking about the city you lived in Ukraine, you should tell her something like "I loved living in Kharkiv..It's one of those cities with unique Soviet history. I've read so many novels that are based in this city". Now you have given her follow up such as the novels you read about the Soviet era.

Every single thing a girl says to you gives you material to work with. When you work on the materials this way, you'll naturally jump from topic to topic.

When she tells you something, make assumptions and ask questions if necessary to take out further information from her so she expands a topic, offering more of her thoughts. The easiest way to do so is to have genuine interest in the topic and her opinions on it.

Conversational Topics

There are certain topics of conversation are better suited to women you want, most probably within the age range of 18 to 30. These topics are pets, travel, relationships, hobbies, events, books, movies and fitness. You should avoid topics such as politics, religion and long conversations about careers. She wants to be attracted to you, not bored.

Lead the conversation onto topics which allow you to spice it up with fun, sexual misinterpretation, feelings and emotions. You can use these topics in general;

Hobbies

Music
Sports
Weird Hobbies
Talents

Favorites

Movies
Actors
Genre of movies
Music
Concerts
Color
Favorite color to wear
Favorite place
Color of her stuff
Food

Pets, Animals

Dog or Cat?
Childhood pets

Which animal she identifies

Work

Your life in 5 years
You own ideal business
Why are you doing this?

Money

Love or wealth?
If you could buy anything, what would it be?
Work or do your own business?
What would you do with a million dollars?

Childhood

Favorite cartoon?
What did you want to be?
Favorite toys as a kid
Favorite pet
Favorite friend

Travel

Countries you want to visit
Countries you have visited
Greatest vacation ever

Embrace Silences

Cost guys try to fill a conversational space by talking. They keep talking, they don't shut up. They get afraid that if they go silent the girl will get bored and leave.

In fact, you need to listen in order to be heard. That's why I want you to be comfortable with silences. It's a great projection of your confidence. And not only be comfortable with silences, leave silences deliberately. Use silence to build sexual tension by looking into her eyes, smirking warmly to her.

At the beginning you might be doing 90% of the talking and that percentage will decrease as she participates. Until then, make sure you are talking about her. Resist the temptation to fill all the silences.

Always try to find a way to turn the conversation onto her and leave silences to sexualise her with your eyes. Soon she'll open up to qualify herself to you.

Energy Match

Women usually prefer to have pretty much zero input into moving a seduction forwards, preferring that the man takes the lead and thus all of the responsibility.

If you stopped a girl she can leave at any time without losing anything. If she doesn't choose that option, she wants you. Keep going forward. Do not read too much into the responses a girl is giving you in the first minute. Don't get excited by a positive response and don't get angry by a negative or no response.

The first minute of her behaviour has very little relation to whether you get the girl. As long as she's standing there, she wants to fuck. Keep going. Keep wanting her. Keep pushing. Keep flirting. Keep making assumptions. Maintain your good masculine presence with hungry looking wolf eyes, steady slow vocal tone and a light playful unaffected vibe.

You can pretty much say anything as long as you are comfortable with non-verbals. She's reading your vibe, not your reasoning skills or conversational skills. When you are in a two way conversation where she knows your intent, woman will subconsciously ask herself if she has a chemistry with you or if she feels herself good around you.

Don't try hard to impress. Don't try to be logical or cultured. You just have to be light and carefree. You are not leading it anywhere. Once you are both talking about a substantive topic, keep to it for a while.

Don't try to jump around introducing new topics. Just keep the conversation flowing using assumptions. Show genuine enthusiasm in the subject and direct it in ways which satisfy your interest. It's best to just embrace the free-flowing spirit of conversation and keep yourself firmly in the now while fucking her with your eyes. The eyes are your power, so put that into her. As I said over and over again, imagine fucking her in every position.

You don't have to be smooth. Your interaction with her may be lacking in fun. It doesn't even have to involve being social. You don't even have to like each other intellectually. As long as your energies match, she will start to give back. When she starts to give back, you will understand that your energies match. She will be asking you personal questions.

If your energies don't match she won't respond to you as you expect and you will feel that she wants to go. In this case let her walk off without even taking her number.

What you want is the girl you know your energies match. When you find out that your energies match, you know she is attracted to you and you gave her enough comfort to trust you. Now you can go with letting her qualify herself and eventually to the escalation.

Open Yourself

Girls get attracted to men all the time. You can approach a girl, have a great sexual conversation with her and she may be attracted to you. You may be a hundred percent sure that she likes you. However, she gives you her number, she leaves you and forgets about you in a minute.

How does that happen? That happens because you miss making with her real authentic connection.

The word connection in my own experience means "to connect your authentic end to her authentic end". The more honest you are, the deeper and stronger the energetic wires of connection will be.

The problem here is that in most cases a man wants to connect to a woman, in order to get something from her, so the connection is fake. She feels like the guy will "pump and dump" her. This state of being alongside your intentions do not facilitate connection.

The key is vulnerability as I wrote before. To facilitate connection, you have to first be open and honest about yourself with her, combined with a genuine curiosity for her as an individual and most importantly raw unashamed sexual desire to her. Once you get real with yourself and begin to speak honestly about how you feel about her, your flaws, what you want, and what you think; the floodgates begin to open. Here are the three things you should consider.

Know Your Intentions

So let's say you met with a beautiful girl, you have good vibe between each other and now you definitely know she is attracted to you. Be clear about your intentions. On practical terms, ask yourself these basic questions when it comes to connecting with her.

What are your intentions for her? What are your intentions for women in general? What are your intentions for the day? What are your intentions in the way you live your life?

There is no difference in importance levels, between your intentions with women and life. See every facet of who you are as an opportunity to get really clear on where you stand and how you show up in every way. The more clarity you have, the more you can connect with her.

Do you want to have really quick sex with her and move on to experience another girl? That is fine. It's not bad if it is what you want, and you understand why you want it. Own it, and make no fucking apology for it.

Most people only do what they have been told is right for them by somebody else. Men feel so guilty for having this type of intention and urge, because society has told them it is a bad thing. You know what is best for you. Listen to you. You don't need a relationship to get sex. You don't need to be the rich guy or the good looking guy to get sex.

All you need is to be real with her. That doesn't mean you will pump and dump her. It means you really like her and you want to share your energy with her without thinking of getting into a relationship. If your intention is to share something with the possibility of long term relationship though, then tell her that.

Know what you want first and foremost. For example; I always look for a relationship that I'm the lover while screening girls for same day sex. If I like a girl, I stick to her and always give the R-selected vibe making her know that I can get into relationships. If I find a relationship, I only go out few times a week to train for same day sex. This time I don't take any phone numbers and I let the girl I meet know that I'm not looking for a relationship or dating.

The point I am making, is once you are an authentic person at your core and you mean it with your sexual intent, and you bring love to the table, then you are on your way to create a connection with her.

Be Curious

Being genuinely curious about a woman is incredibly attractive to her. We all want to feel special and like we take up some space on this earth. Being genuinely curious about her allows her to feel this.

Curiosity is the greatest compliment. Ask yourself why you are drawn to her. When you find tell her. Your main focus when communicating with a woman is not to engage logically with her, but instead engage emotionally and sexually. Learn why she does what she does, and how she feels when she does the things she is passionate about. Allow yourself to celebrate those qualities when they come up. Being curious about her creates the connection, she feels it.

Share Who You Are

It is essential that she knows you, who you are and what your own role is in life. Once she feels this from you, then she can begin to see how and where you could fit into her life. This is how human beings assess each other on a whole and connect with each other.

This means you'll ask your more personal questions about her past, present, and future, likes, dislikes and tell about yours. Don't be afraid to ask direct questions but do try to keep them open-ended rather than closed. You don't need to make assumptions in doing that.

After she answers, give your own answers honestly without any fear or shame. Open yourself as much as you can. Don't ever hide who you are. Here are some sample questions:

Her Past

You: What is it like growing up in Ukraine?
You: How were you like when you were little?
You: What's the most impressive place you've been to?

Her Present

You: How do you find living in Kharkiv? Have you always lived here?
You: Do you really like what you do? Is that your childhood dream?
You: If money wasn't an option, what would you do? why?

Her Future

You: Are you going to stay here forever? What's next?
You: Do you have future plans? Any visions?
You: Will you travel soon? To where?

Her Preferences

You: Do you like thrillers? What is the best thriller you've seen?
You: Do you like to read books? What is the last book you read?
You: Do you like electronic music? Why do you like it?
You: Is this your style? Why do you wear these?

Assignments

Approach 20 Women

Approach 20 women as I have written on day 1.

Write Your Daily Journal

Write your daily journal as I have written on day 1.

DAY 21 - OPENING
| INVESTMENT

Let Her Do The Work

At the start, you had to tell her an opener to initiate things. Then you had to bridge opener to a conversation to a sexual and playful conversation that you both enjoy.

Then you realised that she is attracted to you and you opened yourself up to her. Now you see that she is also opening herself to you. She is clearly attracted to you and there is an authentic connection. What to do next?

<u>You have to stop talking and let her talk now.</u>

You already did most of the work by getting her full attention, attracting her and creating a connection she wants to find out about. Now the girl has a sufficiently high estimation of your value, and is enjoying the interaction sufficiently that she's prepared to work for it because she's also attracted.

You don't need to work for her as much as the beginning now. Let her do the work too. Decrease your energy now. It's so important.

Never forget. You are the best thing that has happened to her. Think of yourself as a famous movie producer. Sure you want her because she is beautiful, but is that all? You want some values more than beauty to make her the star of your movie. Now, she has to qualify herself to you. Let her invest in you first, for you to invest in her.

Many guys need a woman so much that they think they must earn her approval but she should never earn his approval. Actually, she has to earn your approval. You cannot fuck any woman who walks, you have to know which qualities you want in a woman except beauty.

From that point you should slow down your speech, have low vocal tone and speak with short sentences while keeping your strong sexual eye contact. You should really screen her. You should give her nods and listening voices that you are listening to her and asking her to tell you more about what she says.

You should also ask her more challenging questions in cases you don't quite agree with her. Challenge her on the reasons why she thinks so. Talking about yourself at this point is usually a bad thing. Trying to tease, role play, projecting sexual energy or playfulness is another mistake.

Don't try to seem disinterested in her. You are not gaming her. Just dial the energy down, respond to her questions with an open but short answers and then immediately turn the conversation back to her. Let her talk. All women love to talk about themselves. She will open more easily if you focus on her and what is important to her.

You Don't Need Her You Want Her

Remember. You are not needy. You are sexual. You don't need her. You want her. Think of it another way. If you needed her, your interaction with her would be something like;

First you approach the girl and give her a compliment. She somehow likes you and she stays. You think you got her attention so you start to talk, tell stories, tease her, make assumptions. You give high energy to her so she feels socially obligated to give some back. Once she gives some energy, you think that she likes you so you give even more energy. Now you get even more playful, you look at her even more sexual, you want to tease her more, you want to get to know more about her.

Why? Because your energies matched, right? wrong! At this point your energies won't match anymore. She will decide that you are a needy guy and nothing can change that decision. She may still give you her number and talk nice but she won't ever return your text or come to a date with you.

However if you didn't need her but wanted her, after she gave you back energy you would intentionally decrease your energy. Your predator eyes would slightly lose her interest. You would speak slowly with low tone and weak eye contact, nodding your head as she speaks. You would talk with her as if you are the interviewer and the interviewee.

When you do this, she will be investing in you by qualifying herself.

Make Her Invest In You
The primary signal that she is qualifying herself to you is that she talks far more than you do. She smiles and responds well, she listens well when you talk, she's asking curious questions about you and her body language is way more active than yours.

They all point in the same direction: she accepts you as her leader and is ready to be led.

Once you are confident that she has invested herself to you, it's time to tell her your statement of interest by inviting to join you on a date, either immediately or at a future time. Idea here is to make your intent clear and put yourself in a position where she can explicitly reject you.

There's no such thing as a "number close". We are not gaming! The only close that matters is sex and we want that today. Everything else is just a waypoint on the route to her friendship. About 10 minutes in the interaction, once you understand that she qualifies herself to you, it's time to lead her to an "instant date".

Always choose to lead her to instant date rather than getting her number. An instant date is when you lead the girl from the location of the initial approach onto a date without separating any time in between.

The key advantage of instant dating is you are maintaining the attraction momentum. She is in your attraction so she has a high buying temperature. So she will be accepting your leadership. This makes it relatively easy to progress to the date.

If you have just took her number, she will wake up the next

morning without feeling your masculine energy. The "love bubble" would has burst and a date with you is just another event in a list of possible activities that face her in the long list of guys who want to fuck her.

If she has a pre-arranged appointment, a flight to catch, lunch with her family; then you should schedule a date for the closest time, preferably the next day. However If she has less important reasons such as she's out shopping or going to meet with her friends later; don't give importance to them. Pretend that they don't exist and go for the instant date.

Remember, a woman prioritize opportunities for successful intimacy above everything else in their life.

To invite her to an instant date you just say "Look, I like this conversation. Have you got ten minutes? Let's get a coffee over there" and start walking towards the coffee shop as if you fully expect her to follow you.

Always make the initial venue seem like it's no big deal. You can say her "hey, there is a cool coffee shop just over there..I've got maximum 20 minutes..come on". That's it. She's spent enough time with you that she knows if she likes you and wants to spend more time with you.

If you make it a neutral question without an expectation of a positive answer, like you are waiting on her to decide, then you are not displaying your masculinity. For example, don't ask her "Would you like to have a cup of coffee?" or "Shall we go somewhere?".

Always lead her like a shepherd leads the sheep. You have to make sure you have a clear plan. Say to her "let's go to x and y" then start moving the momentum in that direction. Make the decision for her. You can use these phrases to invite her to instant date.

You: Look , let's get a coffee over there (and slowly start walking towards the coffee shop)

You: You know what, this is interesting. Let's go sit on the park for a minute (slowly start walking)

You: Hey, that coffee shop over there looks good. C'mon let's sit(and slowly start walking)

These phases apply to a club. In a club you can see taking a girl from her friends or from a dance floor as an instant date. You can tell her like:

You: I like this. Let's go sit on that lounge together (start walking preferably by holding her hand).

You: Hey, there are too many people around here, let's go and sit on the bar over there. Come on (and start walking)

If she can't make to the instant date, just tell her that you like to take her out drink coffee sometime and ask for the number. Be simple and direct. Make it clear it's okay for her to say no. Tell her what you are going to do when you meet. Let her know it will be a coffee date because you will never buy her dinner before she sleeps with you.

If you met her at daytime, text her the same day you met. If you met with her at night, text her next morning. You should use your phone as the tool to set meeting place and time with her but nothing else. Text her about how she is or what she is doing and after that go for setting the place and time you want to meet her.

Don't ever try to talk with her by texting. If she responds to you, she is interested. If she is interested, she will come to meet with you. Trying to persuade her by texting will do nothing to change what she has in mind and will only make your life harder. Even if she wants to talk with you by texting, cut the interaction short, and go for the date.

Here is an example of how your texting has to be.

You: Hey, it's John, what's up?
Her: hey, I'm fine, how are you?
You: I'm also fine, having a busy day.
Her: yeah me too.
You: Let's meet tomorrow at starbucks near the train station, at 18:00 after work.
Her: oh, ok let's meet. Let's make it 18:30, I may go out late.
You: Cool, see you tomorrow:)

So once you are with her in a date, it's time to fully concentrate on escalating her. If she comes to a date with you, that means she likes you and wants to fuck. Now you may fully focus on escalating her to bed.

Assignments

Approach 20 Women

Approach 20 women as I have written on day 1.

Write Your Daily Journal

Write your daily journal as I have written on day 1.

DAY 22 - ESCALATION | ALWAYS ESCALATE

What is Escalation

Escalation is amping the sexual tension up verbally by talking or physically by touching in general.

Remember that we finished with the investment phase last week. So you may think that you should be escalating the girl after she invests.

This is not a fact. Escalation doesn't necessarily have to take place after you realise that she is attracted to you. In fact, you have to start escalating the girl just after you approach her, by shaking her hands in a way that is sexual.

However, escalation is not the engine driving the seduction until you make her invested in you.

Until you make her invested in you, your sub-communications that come from your clear sexual intent and your authenticity to create the connection will drive the success of the interaction. These will create the sexual tension you want. Once the tension is there, now you can fully focus on escalating her to bed.

That's why this course is called open and escalate. The opening part encompasses more than the approach and the opener. It also includes her attraction, comfort and investment to you. Because only then there will be real sexual tension and the girl will be open to successful escalation.

Otherwise you can touch her or talk sexy anytime but you will come across sleazy if there is no attraction and comfort going on.

Types of Escalation

There are four types of escalation. You can escalate logistics such as moving her closer to a place where sex can happen. You can escalate physically which means you are touching her and being more physical with her. You can escalate emotionally by making the relationship between you and her more emotionally charged. You can escalate verbally which means you can talk about something sexual going on between each other. In our context, we will focus on verbal and physical escalation since these two encompass logistics and emotional escalation.

Physical escalation is your strong sexual eye contact, your gentle touching, then more extensive touching, kissing, leading her logistically and the sexual encounter.

Verbal escalation is what you say to her verbally that will charge her up emotionally and get you closer to sex such as sexual statements, teasing and compliments.

There are some advantages of verbal escalation over the physical escalation. Verbal escalation can be performed in bright public environments without making her think that somebody will see it. You can also deliver your words comfortably while leaning back. However, sex is act of touching itself, and doing physical escalation gradually until sex is more powerful than anything else.

So as a general rule, use verbal escalation in conjunction with physical escalation and when the logistics are unfavourable.

Levels of Escalation

Escalation is done in steps, slowly over time, with the goal of making her progressively more comfortable with your sexuality.

There are three steps for every type of escalation. Light escalation that you do short, almost incidental touches and flirtatious teasing. Medium escalation that you are more intimate and overt with your touches and making a playful sexual talk. Heavy escalation that you touch more intimate areas such as neck, kiss her and talk about sex and making direct sex talk.

Medium Escalation is the key in Open and Escalate Model. It is the passage between Opening and Escalation. You were already using light escalation in the opening part of the model. However, you were just not giving focus on escalation since you had to create the attraction and comfort so she would invest in your by coming to a date. Light escalation was just tool of flirting such as teasing.

Now she is in the date with you and you know that she likes you. She is invested in you. Now it is time to put all focus on medium and eventually to heavy escalation while keeping the mix of flirting and regular conversation on.

In the opening part, flirting and regular conversation was the main building blocks and escalation was secondary. Now, escalation is the main building block, flirting and regular conversation are secondary. So once you know that the girl is invested and you are in the date, you can proceed with the medium escalation.

Keep in mind that every step is based on her comfort level, not on any time limit. Your comfort level as a man is not really an issue. It is the girl's comfort level that dictates the pace of the escalation. That's why you need to limit your escalation according to the location you are, because people feel closer to each other as they change places together.

For example, if you just met with her on the street, you can lightly escalate her. You see that she is invested, now you should lead her to a venue where you will apply medium escalation. To go further into heavy escalation, you should first isolate the girl to more private venue once you gain her compliance.

Having said all of these, be aware that a girl who really likes you will often touch you to help build the physical connection. Whenever the girl escalates, you can "unlock" doing all levels of escalation at any time.

Always Escalate

"Always escalate" is the most important rule of escalation. It's a clear rule of thumb. I learned it the hard way. I used to have the fear that if I escalated too much she would see me as being too forward, creepy, or not a gentleman, so she wouldn't want to see me again. It was completely false and utterly nonsense.

Even if the woman has no intention of sleeping with you, she will sleep with you if you escalate her successfully. Lots of guys talk with women and women love it but their conversations go nowhere. Conversations go nowhere because they don't escalate, they don't show sexual intent and boldness.

You must have the escalation in your mind all the time and you must always escalate if you want to go to bed with her. Otherwise you may have great conversation with her but she will never sleep with you in a million years. By always escalating her, you become a sexually confident and a potential lover in her eyes.

Always escalate. Always always always always escalate. When you're out in public you lightly touch her arms and hands. Lightly brush her legs. Touch her back when showing her something. Talk about sexual topics. When you are alone always go for a kiss, then kiss her neck, licking her and go forward.

Even though she doesn't like it or want it, she is never saying no to you forever, she is just saying no for the right now. Always let the woman be the one that stops you.

Obey The Traffic Lights

When you're escalating the girl you should obey the traffic light signs; Red, Yellow, and Green.

Red light means that she is actively saying no or moving away from you, or changing her body language away from you in subtle or overt ways. This means she is uncomfortable, or un-interested, or both.

Yellow light means she is doing nothing to encourage you but equally she is doing nothing to discourage you. This means she is content to be swept along by you and is apparently comfortable doing so.

Green light means she is giving you interest and responses, escalating on you or actively encouraging you to move the es-calation forward. This means she is aroused and she wants to fuck you.

Most guys escalate on green lights. They basically look for subtle or obvious permission from the girl that she likes him and wants him to do it. This is by far the most common mis-take that men make when trying to progress an interaction forward with a woman they are sexually interested in.

It comes from a lack of experience of what women want and from low sexual self-esteem about their own attractiveness. It is a social construct that "it is not okay to hit on women without their explicit permission because women find this offensive or socially unacceptable" which is nonsense.

Men who are good with women escalate on yellow lights, which means they escalate on compliance. If she complies, assume she is happy with the situation and escalate. For example; if you are touching her hands and she is not removing, go for the arms. If there is no obvious negative interest or discomfort, then you can always escalate.

Women usually prefer almost no input into moving a seduction forwards. She prefers the man to take the lead and therefore taking all of the responsibility. In fact, she uses phrases such as "swept off their feet" or "taken".

Her passive role allows her to not only test your confidence but also her interest in you. It means she can back out at any stage if she changes her mind. It also means that she can't be labeled as a slut because she is not expressing her interest overtly.

This way, she can judge your confidence, sexual self-esteem and if you are experienced with women.

One Step Back Two Steps Forward

When you escalate you need to be in the moment and get turned on yourself but what you must not do is become too excited about the result.

You must be control of your sexual desire. Having strong sexual desire is attractive but having an out of control sexual desire is unattractive. Getting carried away in a club or in any public place puts too much pressure on her.

She may think that you are not showing any manners and treating her like a piece of meat in a public place. She may be afraid that her friends will see her.

So what do you do to make her comfortable?

You take two steps forward and one step back approach. For example, if you're touching her arm, you give her a kiss on the cheek. Then you pull away for a minute or two and next time you go for a kiss on the cheek, then progress to the lips. Two steps forward, one step back. Always control where she is at in the interaction first. Then lead her.

What most guys do is "grab and hold". For example, she seems close to you, so you hold her hand. Finally we've finally got contact! you think. So, you continue to hold her hand. You don't want to give up this level of closeness and touch. After 15 minutes of holding she withdraws her hand and you're panicked as if you've blown it.

A major problem with "grab and hold" is that it's obvious what you're doing. And because it's obvious, she's going to put the brakes on.

Consider another example. So you're seated next to her in the bar, and you get your hand on her thigh, and she lets you keep it there. But when you start to move your way up, she puts your fingers back to the top of her thigh again. When you compare it with two step forward one step back, you put your hand on her thigh for a moment, then slide back down to her knee.

She gets a little charge from your hand on her thigh for the first time in the bar there. But then it's back to your hand on her knee. When you first put your hand on her thigh, she feels "Should I let him do this?"... followed by, "Ok... he took it away," once your hand is back to her knee.

Had you only left your hand there, she would've been stuck wondering whether she should let you leave your hand on her thigh. Eventually she'd likely have decided, "Okay, he can keep it there, but no more intimate than that." Yet when you move it away, the question of, "Should I let him?" is interrupted, and replaced with disappointment that she no longer has the option of letting you.

A little later, you'll touch her on a part of her thigh closer to her panties then return back to leaving your hand on her thigh. The same process repeats in her mind. That process of "Should I let him?" interrupted when you move your hand and replaced with disappointment at your touch disappearing.

Because you do not give her time to answer "Should I let him?" you are not giving her a chance to figure out exactly where she wants to draw the line at. And because of this, you're able to move a lot more rapidly with her while controlling the sexual intensity and compliance.

Never Force Yourself To Escalate

Pickup artists see every single escalation like a routine. This means that they create a scenario for each escalation as it happens naturally and smoothly. You can memorize all the scenarios and try to apply them at the right time, and it may work a couple of times but in the long run it will be perceived as unnatural.

We are not pickup artists. Being an authentic man is about being able to escalate without the girl resisting it. The best way to do that is actually to get aroused yourself and so what you feel to make her aroused. You shouldn't think like "yeah I did hold her hand now I should go for the arms". You should go like "I feel the tingling sensation in my dick when I hold her hand, how it would be like to hold her waist now".

Escalation must come from a genuine place inside you, rather than a forced act. Get really "in the moment" and get turned on yourself. What you must not do is become too excited about the result. By getting turned on you are localising your excitement to her. Girls like to feel desired, it turns them on. Remember the golden rule; she feels what you feel.

You Never Lose a Girl By Escalating

The main worry men have is that their sexual offer will insult the woman and he will be rejected. Yes...this will happen, but in most cases she won't be rejecting you, she will be rejecting your offer to escalate to sex.

I may have messed up two or three interactions by escalating but I never lost any one of them. However, I lost dozens of women by not escalating or escalating not enough. You may not believe me but I guarantee you that you will learn it hard way.

Women want to get fucked too. They want to be raw dogged and bite the pillow in ecstasy of pleasure. Unfortunately a number of factors keep their inner slut at bay, namely social pressure, being branded as "easy" or "slut".

If a woman is on the hunt for a monogamous relationship they will hold on to their chastity as a bargaining tool. They will make the man work for that pussy, especially if you are giving K-Selected signals. This says, "Hey, I'm not cheap. I'm a good girl. I'm a relationship material. I'm your potential wife. You can not get sex that easy."

I know guys that are very attractive to women that never escalate for sex on the first date. These guys are "relationship material." This strategy is absolutely fine. It's the charming gentleman or nice guy approach. The problem here lies in experience. The inexperienced man looking for relationship material is too afraid to escalate out of fear of rejection, or insulting the woman and blowing it. If you wanna go that way, you will wait and wait and wait to have sex.

If you want sex fast, I challenge you to blow it! A woman

will never come out and tell you her magic number of hours needed before sex. And until sex occurs you will never truly bond with your woman. Until sex, you have no relationship. A woman needs to know you are willing to go the distance.

As I said before, a woman will usually forgive a man for pushing too hard but never for failing to push hard enough. If she has any sexual interest in you, you'll probably lose her by not escalating. Because if you don't do it, she won't do it for you so there will be no chance of sleeping with her.

Fear of escalation is no different than the fear of approaching her. Do not fear rejection because you really lose nothing by trying and in fact, her estimation of you goes up because escalation (and approach) shows her your confidence and balls. View escalation as going for what you want. A woman wants to see this within you. If she is enjoying to be with you, and she is neutral or responding to your sexual advances, it clearly means that she wants to fuck.

You Are Getting Laid Today

I don't teach you to necessarily have a girlfriend. I teach you to get sex as fast as possible. In fact, I am trying to take you out of the boyfriend category by making you an R-Selected man. When you do that; you can become the boyfriend as you wish and I guarantee that she will love you for yourself, not for your money, status or looks that you may lose one day.

Why am I doing that? Because R-Selected man always escalates and wants her now, not next date or after starting a relationship. R-selected man non-verbally tells her that he is an adventure but not necessarily a boyfriend. When a girl accepts that, she will be with you for sex, but nothing else.

So she has to understand what you are offering. The opening, the bold way you stop her on the street and imposing her your sexual vibe is half of the story. The rest of the story will come from the way you escalate by physically and verbally sexualising her.

First and most important, you have to believe that you are getting laid today. When you meet woman a girl on the street or a club you only have to think of taking her to bed that day, but not tomorrow. Getting her number should mean nothing to you because you are not there for tomorrow, you are there for now. She has to feel that at any moment she can be taken to your house by a taxi.

Obviously, sleeping with a girl you just met is not common, and require meeting a girl that you have a natural chemistry combined with beneficial logistics. The Idea here though, is to give her the clear understanding that you are not the guy she should necessarily put in a boyfriend category. You are an adventure guy, you are there to fuck her now and she can have sex with you even she has a boyfriend. She has to consider this possibility and see the adventure of pleasure laid in front of her.

Touch Her As Soon as Possible

When it comes to touching a girl, it's always best to do it early. This is because it becomes more difficult to do as time goes on.

This is why you should do it early and make it seem as normal as possible. You can start off by making a handshake when you first meet and holding her hand a little bit longer. You can touch her on the elbow or upper arm while trying to make a point. These are the easiest ways to start touching.

You can also touch the lower back while you point at something with your other hand. You can also touch the small of her back whenever she moves very close to your side. The quicker you start touching her, the quicker you know if she is interested or not interested for any reason. It also stops it from becoming awkward later and will make her more bold in touching you.

Make It Fun

When she is smiling or laughing, she is carefree. She is not nervous and having a good time. Any physicality you do is more likely to be accepted by her if you do it when she is already having fun. So make it fun.

When you make it fun, even the most awkward things you may do will be accepted as fun. You can just grab her hand and she may find it too fast. If you make it fun you can always smile or joke about her reaction. But if you are serious it's likely that it won't be for your benefit.

Another benefit of being fun is finding an excuse to touch her. Making excuses to touch her work very well if you use them in a fun conversation. For example; if she is a naughty girl for some reason, tell her that your mother used to slap your hand when you were naughty..hold her hand and slap her hand gently. Don't make the excuses up by the way, they have to be real.

Look Her Eyes When Touching

When you are touching her always look at her eyes. Don't look to the place you are touching. You may want to touch her hands or arms but if you look at the place you touch it will look awkward. So continue looking her eyes and touch her as if it's the most natural thing to do in this world.

Be Close To Her

In all escalation steps you should be or sit close to her. This makes her comfortable to you and lets you touch her easily.

If you met her on the street, you should talk with her as close as possible. When you go to an instant date you should sit opposite but close to her in a small table. When you go the second venue, you should sit next to her so you will be able to kiss her before taking her home.

It is the same idea in a club or bar. When you meet, you should be looking directly to her as close to her as possible. Then you should aim to take her to a bar where you can easily touch her legs and then to a couch where you can kiss her.

The best way to make sure you will be close to her is to plan your venues beforehand. Always know the coffee shops and bars you will take the girl to sit with her closely.

Touch Her Gently

Always touch her gently and slowly. Don't rush your touch as if you are grabbing her. Try to just let your fingertips caress her skin. Avoid sharp and quick movements.

Softer and smoother touches are relaxing and sexy. Caress a woman gently and softly, like she is made silk. Your can give compliments while you are caressing her. This can make the caressing seem even more intimate and special.

When you hug her, gently stroke her back with one hand as you hug her. If she seems to like this, then you might reach up to her face with your other hand and gently stroke the side of her cheek.

Always Be Leading

Remember you stopped her to fuck her. And remember women love to fuck. They scream so much during sex because they really enjoy it. So until she fucks you she'll try to play the role of nice girl even though she'd just love to find a guy who is down to fuck her and make her scream. She's waiting for your lead. She needs you to tell her it's okay to go down this path.

You need to believe in and imply her in every chance that when a man meets a woman he likes, then sex is the most natural thing in the world. Forget about if she likes you or not. Think about yourself all the time. She feels what you feel. If she calls you out for being too forward, tell her that you are a man and when you are with a woman you like, it's very normal to act sexually.

Always be unashamedly sexual and lead her to your bed so she will feel hundred percent sure to fuck you. In life and also with women, nothing will be given to you, you take it yourself by hustling. <u>Women want to be led and swept away by a dominant man. It's a woman's dream</u>. Being dominant is first and foremost defined by a man's ability to lead. Think that she is your own object. Take her and lead her.

When you are leading her to sex go to at least two places before taking her home. Doesn't matter if you met her on the street in a club. Always aim to change the physical locations. The reason is because when you go to different places with her, she feels like she has known you longer. It creates trust.

So if you met her in the street, take her to a coffee shop then to a bar before you take her to your house. If you met her in a club, take her to the bar of the club and preferably to a couch in the club before you invite her to your house. Two places is enough.

Especially in the street, what's significant about these venues are you want to be closing the distance between your place and venue. If your house is far away from the city, it is always better to choose the second venue closer to the subway.

Assignments

Approach 20 Women
Approach 20 women as I have written on day 1.

Write Your Daily Journal
Write your daily journal as I have written on day 1.

DAY 23 -
ESCALATION | LIGHT
ESCALATION

What is Light Physical Escalation

You have to start with light physical escalation to break the initial physical barrier with the girl. These are light, sometimes incidental touches that you can use in a public setting.

To use light physical escalation, you don't necessarily have to know that she is attracted to you. In fact, light physical escalation will help you to attract her. When you initiate the physical contact with her, she will get a rush of emotions. As humans we all love to be touched.

If you can do calibrated touches early in the interaction, she will immediately get a rush to find more about you and be more likely to put you in an adventure category. That's why it's best to start light physical escalation in the first place you meet with her and use it until you lead her to the second place.

For example, if you met her on the street you may start by holding her hands. When you are in a club, it may be taking her away from her friends by holding her hand and going to the bar. You have to focus on the most public parts of her body such as hands, arms and shoulders. Your touch should be friendly and playful, the same way that you touch your friends.

It is important to keep it light and do not linger. As long as you keep things playful she will not resist the touch, as opposed to you trying to take something from her.

Now I'm going to write you some light physical escalations I use. Do not memorize them as pickup artists do. Just learn how it's done and improvise them according to rules I mentioned yesterday, such as getting aroused yourself, having fun, one step back two steps forward and the traffic light system.

Hands

Handshake

The first physical escalation you can do is the handshake right after you meet with her. You open the girl and when you see the smile it's time for the handshake. Once you raise your hand, she will going to shake it as an automated response she used to do.

You won't shake her hand like in a business meeting though, you have to actually hold her hand rather than shaking. Your palms face up as if you are going to hold her hand and take her somewhere. You can even caress her hand with your fingers.

Once you get her hand, don't pull away. Just leave it there. Most of the time she will pull away. Sometimes, when she really likes you, she will just forget her hand over there and when that happens it makes the interaction so intense. In this case caress her hand while deeply looking her eyes. I do kiss her hand if I see clearly feel the energy.

You: My name is John (raise your hand for the handshake)
Her: I am Sally
You: Nice to meet you sally (hold her hand..if she doesn't remove it lightly caress her palm)

Hand Slap

When the girl says something naughty or something about herself that makes her lazy, you can playfully use hand slap. In this case just hold her hand and slap her hand slowly saying her "naughty."

Her: I don't have courses today in the university, that's why I'm walking out.

You: oh really, but it's the end of the year, don't you have to be at home studying.
Her: yeah, but I just don't want to
You: but you said your parents are paying for your tuition fees.
Her: Yeah they do
you: It's too bad..you are just a naughty girl...naughty, naught girl..this is what my mother used to do to me when I was naughty (hold her hand gently and slap)

Nail Check

Almost all girls somehow care for their nails by colored nail polish or kinds of manicure. After delivering the opener, generally when you are flirting with her, just take her hand and look at her nails. Tell that you really liked her manicure and ask about it. Then leave her hand. You can even comment if she has nothing on her nails. You can talk about how simple and beautiful they are.

You: hey, I like your nails (take her hand). Is that a french manicure?
Her: yeah it is.
You: did you do it? It's looks very professional (leave her hand)
Her: thank you, I did it at home.

Emphasis

When you first meet a girl, it's important to establish that you're comfortable touching her. Simple things like touching her arm with the back of your hand to emphasize a point in conversation send strong messages. You can also lightly tap her arm or shoulder to reclaim her attention if it temporarily wanders.

Her: Tells about the books she works on.
You: you know you seem like a hardworking girl.. I'm very certain that you will finish writing that book soon(touch her hand)

ANDY SORAKLIS

Her: yeah I will

Arms

Arm touch

Arm touch is about holding her arms with an excuse. It's a great physical touch you can do after the handshake that creates the intensity between you and her. There are many excuses you can tell her to touch her arms but I almost always use the bicep squeeze to start.

Talk about fitness and tell her how you pump your arms in the gym. Then look at her arms as if you are trying to understand if she works out well. Then ask her to squeeze your biceps.

You: I worked out a lot today. Pumped my arms. Do you work out?
Her: yeah I do.
You: Oh really. Let me squeeze your bicep to understand how well you do (squeeze bicep)
Her: I don't have biceps(smiles)
You: No need to be ashamed about your biceps. Look at mine. Hold my biceps.
Her: Yeah I see
You: Hold them (playfully take her hand and put on my biceps if she doesn't)
Her: Yeah they are big.

What Is Light Verbal Escalation

Light verbal escalation is usually talking about topics with sexual undertone and giving her sexualised compliments. Idea is to lightly introduce her thinking sexual thoughts about you. Here are some examples;

Sexualised Compliments

Sexualised compliment is first giving a girl a compliment and then sexualising it. If somebody tells you something about yourself you will be interested in that even if you are not interested in the person. All girls have incredible egos that need appreciation. Complimenting her is a great way to make her emotionally invested in you.

Unlike nice guys who buy her flowers and compliment her to get sex, you will be sexualising your compliment in a "cocky and funny" way. You will also use the words like "ass", "fuck", "tits", "dick", "sexy" rather than telling more polite words nice guys use such as "cute" and "beautiful" or "butt".

Sexual Hair

You: I love your hair, it looks amazing. It makes you look so sexy.
Her: oh really..Thank you.
You: yeah, I would love to see you with this hair when you are wearing short skirts, I would love to look at your ass from behind.
Her: Wow, you are a naughty guy.
You: you make me naughty, your sexual aura makes me think naughty things.

Fit body

You: I love how fit you are. I couldn't keep my eyes off your ass..it has the perfect shape.
Her: oh really?
You: yeah, I actually want to slap it but we just met, I shouldn't.
Her: you shouldn't.
You: Yeah, no I shouldn't slap your perfect ass yet.

Bossy

You: You're a nice girl, but I see a naughty side somewhere in there too.

Her: really?

You: yeah, you walk, you talk and you seem too bossy. I imagine you have whips and chains at home.

Her: Oh no I don't have them.

You: So you have handcuffs right? I would love to get handcuffed by a sexy girl like you.

Intimate Topics

If you are having a conversation about Japanese food, that's less sexual than having a conversation about tattoos. If you are having a conversation about tattoos, that's less sexual than having a conversation about relationships. If you are having conversation about relationships, that's less sexual than talking about how was her first sex.

There are a range of topics that are more intimate and more geared towards sex and you should select the conversation topics considering that. For light verbal escalation, you will talk about relationships and sex without overly stating about sex. These topics may include;

- Most romantic experience
- Weird relationships
- First kiss
- Things she looks for in her partner

You can ask questions like;

You: What do you find most attractive about a man?
You: What do you think you look sexiest in?
You: How do you flirt with a guy when you want to show him you're interested?
You: Have you ever made the first move with a guy? What was it?
You: Do you consider yourself a sexual person?
You: Where did you have your first tattoo?

Always lead the conversation onto topics which allow you to spice it up with fun, playfulness, sexuality, sexual misinterpretation, feelings and emotions.

Assignments

Approach 20 Women
Approach 20 women as I have written on day 1.

Write Your Daily Journal
Write your daily journal as I have written on day 1.

DAY 24 - ESCALATION | MEDIUM ESCALATION

What is medium physical escalation

After she is comfortable with light physical escalation you progress to medium physical escalation. This type of escalation is still playful, but a bit more intimate and overt. You can now go for slightly more private body parts such as her back, waist and legs. At this level longer touches can also be introduced.

However, before you do it is a good idea to perform a short or incidental touch around that area first, to test her comfort level before you go for a longer touch. For instance, you can let your leg brush against hers, or gently tap her thigh while making a point, to see if she would be comfortable with longer touch on her legs.

Medium physical escalation will generally cover the things you will do physically with her between the first venue you sit with her and the second second venue you take her. For example, if you met her on the street and escalated her to a coffee shop instant date, now in the coffee shop, you should do certain physicality to arouse her and escalate her to a bar.

In the first venue you take her, the first thing you do should be making her feel comfortable. You want to make her relax. That's why you don't sit next to her, you sit opposite to her to give her space. Also avoid any physical contact with her at first.

Once you feel that she is relaxed, generally in 15 minutes, you can start with a physical escalation such as eye blink game. In this phase, mostly focus on holding her hands and arms, if she is comfortable, you can go further with touching her legs and so on.

These are the examples of medium physical escalation. Again, do not memorize these as pickup artists do. You have to improvise them to make them natural.

Hands

Eye Blink Game

Eye blink game is a very effective way to hold her hand for a longer time. Look at her eyes deeply and then tell her that you want to play a game that you saw in a TV show. Tell her that you will stare into each others' eyes without blinking. The first to blink loses.

You: Hey, I love how you can directly look me in the eye...let's play a game I have seen in a tv show.
Her: Which game?
You: It's a blinking game. We look at each other and the first one to blink loses. I challenge you!
Her: Ok, let's play.
You: Ok 1-2-3 start (look at her deeply while projecting sexual thoughts)
Her: I lost!
You: Ok, one more time. Ok 1-2-3 start (project sexual thoughts)
Her: You lost now.
You: ok, let's play one final time
Her: ok
You: Give me your hands (gently hold her hands).. can you do it better now?
Her: You are cheating (giggles)

Hand Tease

Look at her hands as if you've seen something on her hands and hold her hands telling how gentle her hands are. Leave her hands after caressing them. For example, you can ask her if she washes the dishes at home while holding her hands. You can continue by asking if you were to prepare food with you she would wash the dishes or not.

You: Hey, how gentle your hands are (hold her hands). They are like the hands of a baby (caress her hands)
Her: Yeah I use hand cream a lot.
You: So you don't wash the dishes (continue holding her hands)
Her: Yeah I don't
You: So if we prepare food together am I going to wash the dishes? You won't wash them with me? (leave her hands)

Hand Comparison

Look at her hands as if you've seen something on her hands and hold her hands telling how small her hands are. Leave her hands after caressing them. Compare your hands with her hands.

You: Hey, how small your hands are (hold her hands). They are like the hands of a child (caress her hands and leave)
Her: Yeah people say that
You: Let me compare them with mine (hold her hand and compare with yours)

Hand Tickle

If you have already held her hand, let's say by eye blink game, next time just hold her hand and ask her if she gets tickled from her hands. Then gently curl one of your fingers, preferably your index finger inwards and gently stroke and tickle your targets palm with it.

Move your index finger in her palm around in circles and up and down. Continue for a minute unless you get a "enough" reaction and then leave her hand. If you try a few times and she continues to retreat, stop and try later, or try something else. Most likely, she will start tickling back and it'll escalate into a full fledged tickle-fight.

You: Hey, do you get tickled from your hands (gently hold her hand and tickle her palm)

Her: Yeah I do

You: you know as far as I know, women love this (tickle her palm even more)

Her: So you do this to all women..

You: I do this to you, I like feeling your body.

Palm Map

If you are a foreigner in the city or you are from a different country she didn't visit, when you are talking about the place you were born, you can show her where it is on the map while holding her hand and using her palm as the imaginary map. You can take her hand and use her hand as map to show your hometown. If you are not a foreigner, then you may ask her where is the most interesting place she has travelled to.

Her: Where were you born?

You: I was born in the city of Chios, Greece. It's in the east of Athens.

Her: There must be many islands there.

You: Yeah, let me show you. Give me your hands (hold her hand). This is Athens, this is Turkey, now the island is just there...I also lived in Turkey...it's here...(play with her hand)

Her: Where is your favorite place?

You: I have been to Cornwall years ago. I loved it.

Her: Where is Cornwall?

You: It's in the UK. Let me show you (hold her hand). This is London, this is Wales, this Plymouth and Cornwall near the sea..(tell more)...and in Cornwall there is secret place I discovered...(continue playing with her palm)..this is Cornwall map and this place is just beneath the mountains over here...

Thumb war

A thumb war is a game you play with her using your thumbs to simulate fighting. The object of the game is to pin her thumb, often to a count of three. The game may look like childish but through the game you are holding her hand for a long time, thus increasing the effect of your touch on her.

Also since it's childish it encourages both of you to be yourselves, thus making a connection.

You can start the game by teasing her like "Hey I'll bet I can beat you at thumb wrestling" Or "I've never lost to a girl at thumb wrestling, wanna take my virginity?". Make fun of her if she wins for being "a tough girl". Make fun of her if she loses for being "a weak girl".

After the shake extend holding her hands a little longer if you liked it. This will have her thinking about the fact that she is getting closer to you.

You: Hey I'll bet I can beat you at thumb war.
Her: It's too childish.
You: come on, I think you are afraid.
Her: Ok (hold her hand)
You: You are a weak girl, you have no chance with a powerful guy like me (continue holding her hand)

Back

Genuine hug

Whenever you feel like giving her a hug, but not when you feel like needing a hug you can give her a hug. It must come from a genuine place inside you, rather than a forced act.

You can give her a hug to reward her when she has done something good or when she said something you really find funny. If she seems cold in winter, you can give her a hug to make her warm. If the club is too crowded you can give her a hug to protect her.

You: You know, I can't hang out with girls who don't give good hugs. Do you give good hugs?
Her: Yeah
You: Prove it
Her: (She gives you a hug)
You: That was weak (Then show her how it is done by giving her a really good hug, heart to heart, get close to her face, look at her eyes and lips)

Hand on her back

When leading a girl somewhere such as dance floor, the second venue such as a bar or a toilet, place your hand on her back when you are indoors.

When you are in a bar or club, you can also rest your hand on her back to emphasize that you are protecting her from the crowd. Not too high, not too low but right in the middle. If she likes it, rub her back a little. Then you can pass on to her hips.

You: Come on, let's go the Andy's bar just two blocks away from here (hold her back)

Her: ok lets go
You: Let's go, come on! (rub her back)

Knees

Hand on her knee

Put your hand on her knee while talking. Then, when she expects that is all you will do you, squeeze her knee when making a point in the conversation.

Stomach

Flat stomach

While you talk about fitness you can give her a compliment on her flat stomach as you slide your hand over it. When you do this you can get a sense for whether she would be comfortable with a longer touch around that area, such as having your hand around her waist.

You: Hey, you look like you are working your abs out.
Her: Yeah.
You: Let me check if they are strong(touch her abs)
Her: yeah
You: I love your flat stomach. It's so hard for a girl to get a flat stomach. You have to be careful what you eat and exercise. But it's worth it because I think it's so sexy..I like the lower abs(caress that part)...it's hard to remove the fat over there...the side laterals are easier(caress that part)

What is medium verbal escalation

Medium Verbal escalation not only covers a playful and sexual talk, it also covers you penetrating into her world with your frame. The purpose of it is to imply that you are an adventure and you will fuck her today and you will do that regardless of who she's looking for.

It will mostly include sexual statements you make to her, role playing, future projection and breaking her frame.

Sexual Observations

You have to compliment her as a sexual being. Women love these kinds of specific comments. Just let her see how she makes you feel and what your intent is.

You are not gaming her. These comments should be your genuine sexual admiration. Figure out physical attributes you like about her and tell them in a way that conveys sexual interest and shows appreciation to her. Here are some examples;

Passion for work

Get her talking about her job or hobby. At the peak of her enthusiasm, when she finishes the story and looks at you , comment sexually.

Her: I will be managing a new store next year, I will sell the most stylish clothes.
You: I like how you are passionate about your work, I think it's very sexy.

Her dress

Notice something you like about her clothes then feed it back to her with a sexual comment.

You: the style of your dress is nice. It hugs your figure and bring out the curves. I find that very sexy

You: I love the patterns in your skirt, the colors fit with your sexy tanned legs.

You: I love your dress and your short hairstyle. It opens up your neck. It makes me want to kiss it.

Her eyes

Tell what you like about her eyes.

You: I love your eyes. I think you can see a person's character in their eyes. You have big eyebrows too, they make you look so sexy.

Future Prediction

Paint the picture of a future scenario that involves you both romantically and then describe it in vivid detail. It should be playful. Put your imagination into it.

At this level do not put actual sex into the story or it'll seem like you are just trying to get sexual validation from her. Make the story subtly sexual. You can build anticipation of sex, then refuse it. For example;

Perfect vacation

You: I like Cesme. There is a beautiful beach out there. I wish I could be there now.
Her: I also wish I could be on a beach now.
You: Yeah, me too, imagine we are lying there together.. I'm looking at your body, to your bikini. Your long legs, you know...and I come next to you..I can see your chest rising and falling as you breath heavily...I know what you're thinking..then...I leave you and go fishing...

Castle Sword Fight

You: Do you like castles?
Her: yeah I do
You: I remember a castle I visited in Spain. There were rooms where masters used to have a sword fight. Cutting and removing a part of opponent's dress meant getting points.
Her: Yeah, interesting.
You: I imagine being with you in Spain now, in that castle at this time of night. We are drinking wine and playing that sword game. Getting naked, step by step. You would kill me trying to cut my dress.

Sexual Role Playing

Sexual role playing is introducing her a scenario where you two are clearly having sex but not mentioning about it. For example; you may be talking about you two being the most popular guy and a girl in the school and you finally found each other. You may mention how everyone is so jealous of you and you have a strong sexual energy between each other.

Make sure that the role play you use isn't going to insult to her. You can't role play about turning her into a prostitute. Focus on making it fun.

Secretary and boss

You: I might like to hire you as my secretary but I require short skirts. Any problems?
Her: No problems, I guess..
You: you know we may work overtime in the evenings too..

Teacher and student

You: You know I visualize you as my naughty student and myself as the innocent teacher.
Her: Oh that's interesting.
You: You are the most successful girl in the class because we meet secretly after the class and study together.

Thief and decoy

You: Let's rob that bank!
Her: How?
You: Ok..you will help me get into the bank by seducing the old guard. We will then steal the money and run away to our cabin in the forest to celebrate it until the morning.
Her: What are we going to do in the cabin?
You: Of course we will have sex on a bed full of money. (even

though it's early in medium escalation, if she asks these kinds of questions, don't be ashamed to talk like this)

Breaking Her Frame

People follow their frames. Just like a boxer who thinks he is the greatest acts accordingly, a woman acts according to her frame. Of course it differs depending on the woman, but you'll encounter one particular frame over and over again. That is "I am the prize".

When she wants something, she gets it. When she doesn't it goes away. All because she is good looking.Whether the man who is providing her is her father, boyfriend, teacher or husband; she is used to get emotional and financial things from men.

The frame she is starts when she is little and it goes to make her very, very good at two things. Getting validation and things from men, stoping men from fucking her.

In reality, all women have a weak frame. Because she had never faced unforgiving world that men face every day. She doesn't have to earn money, she doesn't have to take rejections, she doesn't have to go through frustration. Most women, especially hot young ones, have a frame that has been extremely inflated by beta males, especially ones in online dating. They are just unprepared for situations where they really have to work for something. Such as being with a R-selected man.

This should be your only path to fucking real beautiful women. You really, really don't have to give a fuck about her frame. In reality, she is surrounded by successful man and %95 of the time she will have a boyfriend. To make the difference, you have to get her off her "I'm the prize" frame.

In the investment phase of the opening part, you didn't continue investing on her after you realized that she liked you. That made her qualify herself to you. Now, in escalation, you will become more clear and open about who is the boss. You will make her sure that she won't be fucking a guy who sees her as the prize anymore.

As long as she thinks she is the prize, you won't be on the path to fucking her. So, the stronger you hold your own frame, the better you will be taking her own frame over.

First of all, know that you are the best thing that has happened to her. I'm not talking about you should be the prize. That frame of mind is weak. It should be your own realisation in your gut that you are valuable and you are entitled to her. You will desire her but as I said before, it shouldn't come from your need, it should come your sense of entitlement to her as well as your vulnerability. Just like a child wants the toy.

Second, know exactly what you're after. Know what you want. If she knows what she wants and if she's more sure of what she wants than you are, you lose. For example; she may have the frame; "I want to find a boyfriend", "I want to find a husband", "I want to find a guy to have sex" or "I don't want anybody right now". If you are certain you want to hook up with her, then you can make your frame dominant.

Third, remain unaffected when she tests you. Women with strong frame will test you if she wants one thing and you want another. She's going to try to pull you into her frame or see how serious you are about yours. When this happens remain unaffected, and continue to put your raw sexual energy and solid frame on her.

When you do these, you may change the frame of "No, I will never ever have sex with you" to, "Ok, we can have sex". Here are some examples:

I am not that kind

Her: You are taking things too fast, we just met.

You: well when a man likes a woman he should be sexual.

Her: why are you thinking like that? we are not animals.

You: That's right but I am definitely not a gentleman. By the way, why are you so sexually closed? when was the last time you had sex? Or are you a virgin? hmm...

Let's be friends script breaker

Her: I'm not looking for someone in my life now, I just want to be friends.

You: Yeah, that's why I invite you to my house..we'll just have a friendly dinner.

Her: No I won't come to your house.

You: Ok, don't worry we won't have sex...I will never sleep with you, we will be friends.

I want a boyfriend

Her: I want a committed relationship. My last relationship was 4 years long. I can't go this fast

You: I personally don't want to lose my freedom and independence in a committed relationship, however if I find a girl who can blow my mind, I can settle with her. Are you the girl who can blow my mind?

Her: so you don't want a girlfriend? You just want sex.

You: (Look at her eyes) Yeah, I just want sex now. Hot passionate sex, and more hot passionate sex and more hot passionate sex with you. That will only open up the possibility of a loving relationship. Wouldn't you want a relationship like that?

I have a boyfriend

Her: I actually have a boyfriend

You: No wonder, every hot girl has a boyfriend. Don't worry, that's ok for me, I don't try to find a girlfriend. I want someone I can enjoy being with me without the commitments, heartaches and pressures.

Her: really?

You: Yeah. Committed relationship take too much freedom

from a person. You can feel totally free with me, no one will find out that we are spending time together.

I'm married

You: Don't you think marriage is that it makes cheating each other a necessity?
Her: really?
You: yeah, don't you know why many women get married?
Her: no.
You: it's the only way to get access to resources of a man and have children...and of course be free all day to do what they want with other men, the ones they really want.

Leading her to second place

Once she is responding to your medium level escalation you should take her to another place. That creates the trust and gives her more comfort. That place has to be a more intimate place where you can pass onto the next step, heavy escalation. It can be a non-busy pub/cafe that has tables with couches or a couch if you are in a club.

The most important thing is that you have to find a way to <u>sit next to her</u> in order to pass on to heavy escalation. That's why sitting on a couch with her is important and you have to plan the venue you will sit next to her before. The way you sell her the second venue is to create a picture of you two going somewhere nice to drink a beer or just sit comfortably.

Tell that the venue is great, they have great drinks and very comfortable seats. Sell the venue. If she says no, stay in the place and in 5-10 minutes insist again. If she doesn't want it, set up the date next time in that venue.

If she says yes, you have to take her to the place of that venue where you can sit next to her. Make sure you go to a place where there is a table with a couch on one side. Make sure place is not crowded and people won't openly see when you are kissing. Let her sit down on the couch first and sit next to her like it's no big deal. Put your jacket on the chairs before she sits to guarantee it.

If she just sits on the chair, sit opposite of her on the sofa, continue escalation such as holding your hands and 10-15 minutes later tell her that you want to be close to her, then hold her hand and invite her next to you.

Leading her to a pub

You: I know the coolest pub in the city just over there, let's go there and grab a quick drink.

Her: I don't drink at day time

You: You don't have to. Let's go (take her hand and stand up)

Her: Ok, is this the place? (she enters the place)

You: Yeah, that place looks great (put your jacket on chair, ask for her jacket and put there..and sit together on the couch)

Sitting next to her in a pub

Her: I want to sit on these chairs (she sits)

You: ok..as you want (wait 15 minutes)

You: You know, this talk is becoming like an interview, I want you to come sit next to me..come on(hold her hand and gently make her stand up and sit next to her.)

Her: Oh...ok..why not

You: that's better

Leading her to a couch in a club

You: Hey, I'm a little bit tired of standing like this in the bar, let's sit on the couch over there (hold her hand and start walking)

Her: ok, let's sit (she walks)

Assignments

Approach 20 Women
Approach 20 women as I have written on day 1.

Write Your Daily Journal
Write your daily journal as I have written on day 1.

DAY 25 - ESCALATION | HEAVY ESCALATION

What Is Heavy Physical Escalation

When she is comfortable with medium escalation you can move on to heavy escalation.

Since you changed places with her, she is going to feel much more comfortable being with you and she will be more receptive to your sexual advances. Heavy physical escalation includes longer hand touches and more intimate areas such as her legs, neck, ears, hair and lips.

Heavy physical escalation does not include erogenous zones such as her breasts, crotch or inner thighs. Those areas are not paid any direct attention and they should be done in private, not in a venue where people are.

You must be sitting close to her. Otherwise you won't be able to do heavy escalation. That's why always plan your venue and how you will sit close to her as you did in medium escalation phase. Since you changed venues you can start with medium escalation, do more incidental touches before you go for more overt ones. Always test her comfort level before you go for a longer touch.

Hands

Hand hold

When you are leading to the second venue in the street or to a couch in the club, hold her hands. Hold for a longer time frame such as 5 minutes and then leave. Same applies when she accepts coming back to your house, hold her hand as if you are holding your girlfriend's hands. You may also caress her palms.

Hand play

When you are sitting close with her in the venue, just take her hands and play with them as she is your girlfriend. Let your fingers play with her hand. Don't look her hands. Your conversation should not reflect what you are doing.

Shoulders

Arm around shoulders

After she accepts to sit next to you, slide your hand along her shoulder and let it rest there in a 90-degree angle as if she is your girlfriend. Then in 3-5 minutes leave your arm and in 10-15 minutes put your arm again. It is protective and shows a strong masculine presence.

If she gets uncomfortable just smile. If she doesn't lean in to you, don't get affected. Just continue putting your arms around her until you kiss her.

Hair

Hair Smell

When you are sitting next to her, just smell her hair, leaning closer to her neck. Tell her how great her hair smells. Talk about her hair.

You: I love how your hair smells (hold and smell her hair and leave)
Her: It's just my shampoo
You: It smells great when mixed with your own beautiful smell.
Her: no it's just my shampoo
You: No it's not and I love it, let me get it more clearly (breathe in her smell getting closer to her neck)

Hair Play

Run your hand through her hair or twirl it around while looking into her eyes. Play as if she is your girlfriend. Tell her that you like her hair. To see if she would be comfortable with you touching her hair, you can lead up to it by brushing a stray hair out of her face.

You: I like how curly your hair is (take her hair and start playing)
Her: It's my natural hair
You: I love when women don't ruin her natural hair (continue playing with her hair)

Face

Face Stroke

Lightly stroke her face with your finger while looking into her eyes.

You: I like your smile, when you smile your cheeks get red (caress her cheeks with the back of your hands)

Chin Stroke

Lightly stroke her chin and tell her the animal archetype you told her.

You: squirrel as I told…cutest ever (stroke chin)

Lips

You should be in a very close proximity to kiss her. To initiate kissing try placing your finger just underneath her chin and pulling her mouth towards yours. Don't use too much tongue. Kissing should be light and short at first. You should be the one to pull away. Kiss is meant to build more tension and arousal to move to the next step

Magic Kiss

After some initial heavy escalation such as smelling her hair or biting her neck, look at her eyes and then her lips and ask her if she believes in magic. Then regardless of what she answers, ask her to close her eyes and kiss her.

You: do you believe in magic? (look at her eyes and lips)
Her: I don't.
You: let's see if you will. I will show you some magic. Close your eyes now...(gently kiss her after she closes)
Her: I didn't expect that
You: that's the magic. You don't expect it.

Surprise Kiss

You: do you like surprises? (look at her eyes and lips)
Her: I do.
You: I have a surprise for you. Close your eyes. (kiss)
Her: I didn't expect that
You: that's a surprise. You don't expect it.

Spontaneous Kiss

You: Do you like spontaneous things?
Her: maybe
You: Are you a spontaneous girl?
Her: I guess so.

You: Let's find out (kiss her)

First Thing You Would say Kiss

You: What is the first thing you would say after you kissed me? (tell while you are close to her face, looking her eyes and lips)
Her: I don't know
You: Well, let's find out..(kiss)

Say Nothing Kiss

Just like in the movies there will be a time she looks like she wants to be kissed. When you feel that, say nothing..just look at her eyes and her lips, get slowly closer to her..look at her eyes and lips and go for the kiss.

Neck and Ears

The neck and ears are very sensitive and erotic areas. Being caressed and kissed the right way can amplify arousal in multiples allowing for smoother escalation.

Once you have kissed her for a bit, move down to her neck or up to her ears. Kiss them gently, while holding her close to you. Alternate between the ears, neck and mouth to gauge which spot gives her the most arousal and generally concentrate on that area, but do not neglect the others.

Depending on how rough you want to set the mood, feel free to throw in some gentle biting on the neck or earl lobe too.

Vampire Bite

After some other heavy physical escalation such as touching her legs or smelling her hair and while you're already having fun, playfully ask her if she believes in vampires. Tell her that you are a vampire and you like to bite nice girls like her. Tell her that you are thirsty and you need blood.

You: hey, do you believe in vampires?
Her: of course no
You: I think you will from now on because I am a vampire.
Her: really?
You: yeah, I am a vampire and I love biting nice girls like you.
Her: don't bite me.
You: but I need blood, I can't help(lean in to her neck, very gently bite and slowly kiss her neck)
Her: but you also kissed my neck.
You: yeah that's my style, I kiss the place I suck blood so it won't ache.
Her: oh really..
You: yeah..by the way your blood is sour.

Neck smell with bite

Notice how she smells and compliment her on the smell saying something on how humans and animals mate by smelling. Use that as an excuse to smell her neck.

You: I like how you smell. Lots of people don't pay attention to smells, but we're still animals, and you'll notice that animals, when they meet, and before they mate, always smell each other. It's part of our evolution. (lean in to her neck and smell her again)

Her: hmm

You: the place we like to smell and get tickled are usually the most sensitive places on the body are often places that don't get much contact with air or light, like the crook of your neck (touch her there very gently)...and one of the best feelings is to be bit right here on the neck.

Her: Oh I didn't know that.

You : how would you feel yourself if I would bite your neck now?

Her: I guess, I would get tickled

You: let's see what will happen (smell and gently bite her neck)

Ear Lick

After you kiss her, start playing with her using your fingers and progress to licking her her neck and ears.

You: Hey, I like playing with you. (walk your fingers up her back from her lower waistline to her neck, brush away some hair from the side of her face, run lines around her ears with your finger, breathe into her ear, lightly lick her ear. Run you tongue up around the top to make her aroused)

What Is Heavy Verbal Escalation?

Tell her you want to fuck her, like it's something very normal to say. The purpose of heavy verbal escalation is to remind her where this is going but as if it's very normal. Your beliefs should constantly impose her the frame that when a man meets a woman he likes, then sex is the most natural thing in the world. If she is with you, she likes you.

Sexual Questions

Tell her that you want to have an interview with her. She's got five questions she can ask you, and you'll answer truthfully. Let her ask her questions and tell your answers, then ask your questions, all sexual.

Fantasies

You: Tell me one of your sexual fantasies?

You: Do you have a crazy fantasies such as role play?

Sexual Experiences

You: Have you ever had outdoor sex?

You: Have you watched another couple having sex? How did you feel? Did you want to join?

You: What's the sexual thing you are interested but haven't had the courage to try?

You: How does it feel when a man comes on your face?

Sexual Outfit

You: Do you have sexual underwear? What are you wearing right now? Or are you not wearing at all? do you not wear sometimes?

You: What do you think you look the sexiest in? Why those outfits make you feel sexy? How do you feel yourself in a sexy outfit?

You: Which part of men you find sexual? which part of me you find sexual? Do you like looking man's ass or arms more? If I had an xray on me which part of me would you look? what would you expect? do you think size matters?

Sexual Statements

Use sexual statements generally after kissing her. Get aroused yourself first and tell her what you really want to do to her without any shame because you are not a provider gentleman, you are a R-Selected lover.

Sexual Outfit

You: I love your legs, I want to see you with short skirts and high heels.

Sexual Warning

You: I'm warning you, I'm going to do really dirty things to you.

You: Warning, I get very aroused when I drink and I might try to have sex with you.

You: Naughty things will happen to you if you don't run away right now.

Predictions

You: If that's what you like in sex then I can tell that you like doggy style and being hair pulled in bed.

You: I'm sure you are into whips and handcuffs...but I can't find out...you like doggy style with handcuffs or you on top with whips? or vice-versa?

Confessions

You: you don't know how hard it is to keep me from kissing you right now...You made me so aroused. Look at this..look, hold it if you don't believe how crazy I got (take her hand and put on your dick if the place is suitable)

You: I have to admit...I want to fuck you and I want to fuck you hard.

Sexual Whisper

Sexual whisper is a very powerful way to make things even more sexual. You can use it both before and after kissing her.

Smelling her hair

You: I have something to tell you but it's a secret, I'll whisper.
Her: Okay
You:(Lean over slowly and slide your hand behind her neck. Gently grab the back of her hair, put your lips right at her ear and slowly whisper) I love smelling your hair.

Kissing her body

You: I have something to tell you but it's a secret, I'll whisper.
Her: Okay
You: Kissing your lips and neck makes me want to kiss every part of your body.

Making her slut

You: I have something to tell you but it's a secret, I'll whisper.
Her: Okay
You: I'm going to make you my dirty little slut.

Leading her to your house

Once you are sure that she is aroused, and generally spent and hour or hour and a half in the second place, now it's time to sell her the idea of going back to your house.

The best thing is to do is to invite her to cook/present food for her. The key here is to make the food compelling, no big deal and be ready for her beforehand.

Back in the day when I was living in Ukraine alone, I use to boil delicious borsch soup in the morning to eat in the evening. So not only there was food to eat when I came home, I was planning to eat that soup with the girl I would find that day.

Borsch is interesting all over the world, so if a foreigner invites you to eat local food he cooks it gets her attention. You will usually meet with her after work so you will most probably be hungry. She will be hungry too.

I strictly don't take a woman to dinner before sex. Before sex, never eat outside with her. Make the food you prepare compelling and always remind that you will make her eat the food you cook. The food you cook is sex and she knows that. That's your offer. Even if she rejects first time, she may take it later on (just like email marketing).

You can always go for quick delicious dishes but the food has to be home cooked. I used to have a can of pesto sauce and a papardelle pasta for the days I don't cook. It takes just 5 minutes to prepare but fucking "papardelle" and "pesto" words sells it. Even though you can't prepare well, sell what you can prepare the best you can. Idea is to make it fun and interesting so she will be compelled to come to your place.

If she doesn't want to come to your house after asking several times you should give her one, maximum two dates but not more. Take her number and take her to same pub/cafe next time to invite for your cooking again one more time. Repeat the same process of second venue. Don't go to restaurant until sex, don't go to night outs, don't go to movies, don't see friends. Listen to me not your ego because if she leaves you without sex, you won't stay with the money and time you spent for her.

If she still doesn't want to come home after that meeting, just leave her alone. I repeat, leave her alone even she is going to be your wife. Even she is the most beautiful girl you met. That's exact point you make your difference and break her frame. If she ever contacts you later on, invite her to your house directly (meet her in a subway first). Do not go out with her anymore. Make her know that you have done what you could and now it's her turn if she really wants you. If she wants you she will contact you, don't contact her first. She may even call you after months after a breakup or a depression too, so leave the possibility there, don't ignore her or delete her phone number. Stay in your ground.

Invite for borsch

You: You know what..I've cooked the best borsch you ever ate today! It's even better than your grandma's.
Her: really? hard to find good borsch
You: yeah and I want you to taste it! You know I went to bazaar to buy meat on Sunday, and I bought very interesting spices from Ozbek guys and veggies from grandmas. Today, I started boiling the meat at 7 in the morning and it boiled slowly until 12...then...
Her: Interesting...I don't think I can...I have things to do.
You: look, there is no better borsch you've had before,you will always remember that, it's a big loss if you don't eat it today...and you are hungry, I know that...

Her: Is it that good?

You: Yeah, it's that good and there is only way to find out.. come on (stand up and take her hand)

Invite for paella

You: You know I prepare the best paella you can eat in the world.

Her: really

You: I was planning to prepare today, yeah you have to taste that.

Her: I have things to do.

You: look, it's the best of the best, you will always remember that paella and I need your help to prepare, I can't do it alone. I wanted to do it for weeks but I couldn't, today is the day!! Come on, let's first buy some shrimp(stand up and take her hand)

Invite for wine

You: hey, let's continue this at my house, I have nice chardonnay waiting.

Her: no

You: look, it's a real good wine..you will remember that..and I have some grapes too, it will be better than to drink here.

Her: Hmmm...

You: ok let's go, I live just 20 minutes from here we can take a taxi .

Assignments

Approach 20 Women
Approach 20 women as I have written on day 1.

Write Your Daily Journal
Write your daily journal as I have written on day 1.

DAY 26 - ESCALATION | BEDROOM ESCALATION

Don't Think It's a Done Deal!

It's woman's nature to be choosy and stop men from having sex with her. She is exposed to offering of sex since she is a teenager. Everyday in her life, especially in social media, someone tries to fuck her. That realization brings her great power, but it's also hard so she needs a strategy to make all that men stop fucking her.

Her strategy She find reasons to disqualify men Too short. Too fat. Too old. Bad hair. Whatever. The fact that you are in the final venue and you are kissing means she hasn't disqualified you, but don't think it's a done deal yet.

Once she realizes that she's about to have sex, there may be a last-minute resistance. It's her nature. Last minute resistance often come in the form of an insult, disappearing to the bathroom, asking questions that may make you angry or asking if you are a pickup artist.

I learned this the hard way. I was once with a 21 year old hot, very hot blonde. I couldn't even believe how I got so close to her that fast. We were in the bar. We kissed, held our hands, finished our drinks. We knew we would go home to fuck. I was thinking it was a done deal and I knew I found my girlfriend after dealing with that much lower quality girls. Then suddenly she left for the toilet with her handbag. I waited there in the bar alone half an hour, I looked for her couldn't find her, wrote to her she didn't answer. I paid the bill and got so angry that I wrote her a text that she is a bitch, and how dare she does that, etc. She replied in an hour telling me that she doesn't want to see me anymore. Have I not got angry and told those words, I knew would have fucked her.

She may leave you as she left me. She may tell that she doesn't have sex on a first date. She may invent a reason that she needs to get up early tomorrow. She may go quiet. She may even flirt with someone else. You have to know that it's a last minute resistance and she's testing your frame.

Don't fight it, because she wants you to be angry. Don't tell yourself as I told many times "how she can do this to me after all the time and effort I've invested in her!" Never. She has already decided to fuck and it's your last test.

Your response should be to say "I understand" and give a quick plausible explanation without being drawn into a discussion, and then continue pushing on. All she really wants is for you to take responsibility for what's about to happen.

Tell her to finish her drink. Pay the bill. Ask her any questions that don't remind sex. Keep it light. Order a taxi. When the taxi comes walk with her to the taxi. Do not walk too fast. Once you are in a taxi, you passed the last test.

Understand Her Fear

Men fear approaching because the risk of rejection represents a big damage to their ego. Women have the same fear but in another way. She fears that a man will "pump and dump" her. That's her understanding from a "rejection". That represents a big risk of damage to her ego. She thinks she will lose all her power if she gives up sex.

When a girl is entering your apartment after having already kissed you, she knows you're going to try to fuck her. So she will be at most nervous stage in the whole seduction, just like you were when you were approaching her. She's about to surrender her position of power and enter into her powerlessness. She's both scared and excited.

That's why always make her relaxed first. Tell her to take off her shoes and sit as she wants. Offer her both alcohol and non-alcoholic drink and get one for yourself. Leave her alone in your room for some minutes while you prepare food or go to toilet. Don't touch or jump to her right away. Don't look anxious. Be in control of your sexual desire. Once she's comfortable you can start escalating.

I usually start making her comfortable by letting her sit on the sofa. Then I leave the room to heat the food. While the food gets prepared I turn on a movie I like and close the lights. We start looking at the movie and I bring the food when it's ready. We eat and watch movie for half an hour at least. This makes her comfortable.

After finishing our food I put my arms around her shoulder and let her lie on me. While she lies on me I caress her hair. Usually 1 hour into the movie I start kissing her. I let my hand roam her curves. I pull her hair, squeeze her ass. I do everything slowly and gently while we still look at the movie. When I get aroused enough I take her hand and put on my dick.

According to her response I go for her breasts. I take out her shirt, kiss her neck. When she starts to moan I go for the vagina. I rub her vagina until she gets really aroused. Then I remove her bra and let her sit on me. I continue kissing her and at some point I remove my shirt. Then I go for her jeans, remove them and go for the trousers.

I first remove my trousers, then her, not the other way around. When we are both naked, I give my dick into her mouth. Then we continue fucking on the sofa. Usually first sex doesn't go that long. When we finish we continue watching the movie. After the movie I take her to bedroom for the second long sex session.

There will be many cases where she's sitting on your sofa kissing you, but she will block your every attempt to move forwards to sex. This means she wants sex but she doesn't want to give it up easily.

Ignore anything that isn't a clear "No", just back off and go cold for a while. The most important thing to remember here is that you never get angry. If you do, she wins.

Just stop and let her relax for ten minutes then start again. Let your fingers play with her, breath into her ear, softly kiss her neck. Take control and lay strong conviction and dominance onto her.

If she is giving you more resistance, put your finger over her lips, maybe her neck, and continue on. Gently wrest the girl into submission. Like the modern caveman.

Dominate Her

To make a woman deeply fall in love with you, you have to fuck her great. Period. If you are not giving her money and status, then sex has to be the value you are giving her. Only because of sex, she will love you for yourself but not for your money or status you may lose.

When it comes to sex, what is more important than any physical technique is being dominant. Sexual gratification for women is far more psychological than it is physical. Most of this psychological satisfaction comes from being dominated and surrendering control.

Use Her For Your Pleasure

Women know they exist to satisfy the man in their lives. She is there to satisfy you. Men who dedicate themselves to giving women orgasms and oral sex are just sexual providers. Lovers only think about themselves.

In bed you cannot think of anyone other than yourself. If you only pursue your own taste, you will be rewarded with lust. And for a woman, there is nothing more arousing than that. In fact, being an egoist in bed is not enough. You must be a pervert and a filthy rogue. The best woman in bed is a bitch while the best man in bed is a pervert.

You should see her not as a little girl or a goddess to be loved but as a food to be eaten. The biggest compliment a woman can make for you in bed is telling you "nasty pervert". So fuck her like it's your last fuck. Fuck her so good, so hard that she is left with a shaking flesh and sex fluids. Drain her of everything. Then fuck her more.

She shouldn't be able to walk normally after the sex. Forget about fucking her like a princess, you should fuck her like a bitch. Fuck her like a rag doll. Do whatever turns you on. Finish whenever you want. Fuck thinking about your premature ejaculation. Fuck thinking if she likes it. Fuck thinking if she gets an orgasm. Fuck any idea that makes you think about her pleasure. Solely think about yourself. Always but always think about your pleasure, rather than hers. Come whenever and wherever you want to. If she doesn't want it on her face then go for the breasts, making sure your cum gets on her face. Unapologetically.

Don't give her oral sex. Give your dick to her mouth right away. Get physical. Spank her. Pull her hair. Hold her down with one hand. When you change positions, literally pick her up and move her yourself like a piece of meat. Put her body where you want it. When you want to put her on the bed, pick her up and throw her there. Let her know you are enjoying her. Breath heavy into her ear, tell her "I love fucking you".

I repeat. Fuck her like your bitch. However, once sex is finished always give her comfort. Lie on your back like a king and pull her against your chest.

Assignments

Approach 20 Women

Approach 20 women as I have written on day 1.

Write Your Daily Journal

Write your daily journal as I have written on day 1.

DAY 27 - ESCALATION | AFTER SEX

Decide On What You Want

Getting sex from a woman doesn't mean you will be getting sex from her whenever you want in the future. It's obvious that it's much easier to get sex now but after-sex is still a work you have to manage.

First of all, decide whether you want to see her again. You may want to or not, it's your choice. If you have presented yourself as R-selected man and you really didn't make any promises of commitment, she will understand that because she accepted you knowing that.

If this is the case don't make future plans or general talk about hanging out sometime. Also don't tell her you have to get up early or you have to go do something. Have respect for her.

If you want to keep her, you have to give her affection after the sex. Lie next to her, pull her in, softly kiss and stroke her head.

If you want to keep her as your fuckbuddy meet with her no more than 2 times a week. If you see her more she will likely become your girlfriend and once she is your girlfriend, it will be very hard to make her your fuckbuddy again.

Most girls who will sleep with you will want more. If you don't look for a girlfriend, you need to tell them. You will always be honest. Never see her more than two times a week. Try not spending every weekend with her. Your moderate interest will indicate that you are not a suitable boyfriend material but the good sex you give will make her stay.

While others are focusing on providing her presents, emotionally supporting her, going out with her, taking her to vacations and being loyal to her; you must focus on one thing and one thing only; SEX. When you meet you have to give her the best sex she can find at the current time. That's why doing sex exactly opposite of how providers do will help. You will give her the best sex if you focus on solely giving yourself pleasure.

If you want a girlfriend to live romantic things and still have a rotation of other girls then it's the hardest and you may end up losing her. In this case you can do what I do.

When finding a girlfriend I like (not love), I still spend 1-2 hours 3 times a week to meet with single horny women or women who have boyfriends/husbands. I only go for the girls and circumstances that will minimize the risk of losing her. Once I get to know her situation, I tell my situation before-hand and if we agree we have sex knowing out that. Taken women works best for this purpose and makes sex even better than your girlfriend.

Consider If You Want Long Term

Unlike casual relationships, where you can manage to have sex with wide variety a women including the ones out of your league, long term relationships require that both man and woman are at least on the same level.

Happy long term relationships in fact require man being on a higher level than women. 99 out of 100 times, if you are not in a higher level than her, then you won't be happy in a long term relationship.

This is such a big fact that it is the exact reason why humanity proceeds (99% of guys are providers). By saying being higher level, I mean, a woman who wants money will get it, and if you don't have it she will leave you. If she has a higher paying job than yours, that will eventually be a problem. If she's very smart and you don't stimulate her, forget it. If she's from an upper class environment, forget being her boyfriend if you are in the middle. Some women are racist so that may be a problem too.

If you really like the girl and want to keep her as a girlfriend accept the fact that <u>giving sex on the long term is not enough.</u>

There is an exception though for 1 out of 100 times I guess. The exception is called love. Real one though, not the fake one.

Assignments

Approach 20 Women

Approach 20 women as I have written on day 1.

Write Your Daily Journal

Write your daily journal as I have written on day 1.

DAY 28 -
ESCALATION | LOVE

Biological Need

If escalation is amping the sexual tension up, then love is the ultimate escalation. It's the tipping point of sexual tension.

We no longer gather with friends and sing songs after a hard day of work. We no longer gather around a fire and explain stories until the morning. We no longer care about our neighbors. We don't even know them. We don't have friends who we can hug. We can't trust them. We don't have family dinners anymore. Actually, most of us come from a dysfunctional family.

Human animal needs more care than any other animal after the birth. Our mothers give us that care until we grow up enough to take care of ourselves. But what does care mean? If it's a shelter and food, then the government can do that. It also has something to do with emotions.

Scientists in fields ranging from anthropology to neuroscience have been asking this same question for decades. How and why do people love each other? Finally, in a new study, a research team has found a biological standpoint that gives the answer.

Love is the biology of attachment. We know that a group of hormones and neurotransmitters such as oxytocin, vasopressin, prolactin, testosterone, dopamine are involved in developing physiological bonds between mothers and infants. This system also functions in the same way between adults. The system is triggered by physical touch, spending intense social time in contact or near one another, and positive social interactions.

Humans have evolved a system that uses social and physical

interactions, hormones, and the brain, to prime the body to feel closer and more attached to another individual. In the most basic sense, this is the same system common across mammals. The anthropologist Walter Goldschmidt called this "affection hunger".

He suggests that the basic system that acts to bond mammalian mothers to their infants has been expanded in humans to act as a social and physiological bonding system between individuals of all ages and sexes.

This drive of "affection hunger" enables humans to form and experience types of social bonds across a wider range of individuals and with more intensity than in other animals. So one answer to "what is love" can be explained as the biology underlying affection hunger, the ability to form multiple strong social bonds.

Love is a biological need.

This view also suggests that what is called "love" has the same base between parents and offspring, between siblings or other family members, between good friends, and between romantic pairs. Romantic love is not separate from the love a mother feels for her child.

But most people want "love" between romantic pairs to be something different. Culturally we see romantic love as separate from familial or friendship love. Unfortunately, aside from a slightly different pattern of some specific hormones brought about by sexual behavior, there is nothing truly different about romantic love than any other kinds of love.

Biologically speaking that is. Love is a biological need. Does the need have to be towards a woman? Can be, but better not, because if that's the case, she will eventually hate you.

Real Love

What happens if you want her so much but you don't need her? What happens if she feels the same to you?

I think "real love" happens.

What is real love? How it starts? How it's lived? I don't know. I can't explain it clearly.

Meeting with her was like no other. So far I've approached at least 10 at most 15 thousand women and slept with dozens of them. Not only it was different than all others, it was really "love at first sight". It was the exact realisation of the fact that we've been created for each other.

Once our eyes met, that was it. Holding her hands and kissing her in half hour was the most natural thing in the world. A sloppy street stop was our destiny.

When I kissed her, I smelled and kissed her a thousand times. Every night I buried my head in her hair, sleeping in her chest.

Our bodies would fall asleep like cupcake holders. She would wake up like the sun in the morning.

She would put her hand on my penis at any moment and would check from the most trustworthy source that I loved her.

I only liked her hands and her feet. I used to laugh when I heard the sound of her pee in the bathroom.

Everywhere but everywhere we've been to was so much fun. New york, Athens, Izmir, Kayseri, Istanbul, Kiev, Dnepr, Liiv, Paris. We used to walk around all day with laughter and we couldn't care where we are and what we do.

I would want to hurt her if she even looked at another man. I would like to take her everywhere with me in my pocket.

My heart would swell if I saw her walking towards me from a toilet in a stupid restaurant. She was my bunny, I was her bear.

Was I needy? I wasn't at all. I adored her. I wanted her. I dominated her. I incredibly fucked her. I was better than her. I was her master, she was my slave. It was a war, it was a peace. It was a battle. It was dangerous. It was full of pleasure, pain, worries, excitement and fears.

It was exceptionally beautiful. It was so fucking beautiful. As beautiful as the middle ages. As beautiful as the mountains. As beautiful as the galloping horses.

The dream ends one day. The world collapses and everything goes away. If you try to keep it, it goes ever faster. If love doesn't end, it's not love. Suddenly, the spell breaks and you cannot control anything. You recreate yourself from your ashes, and move on.

I don't know. Maybe real love is something like I explained. I don't know. But if there is one thing I do know; that thing is called "fake love". Fucking fake love.

Fake love exist for a reason. All fake loves are built for using each other.

When a girl gets to twenty-five, the education and social pressures that she receives from his family force her to have a good marriage. When she bumps up to a handsome, wealthy, educated and socially high value man, it becomes easier for her to fall in love.

The man also loves his young beautiful bride with her fit body, beautiful clothes, french as a second language, cool friends, cooking abilities and the great taste of art. They finally find what they were looking for. The roles imposed by society work in harmony with each other and a successful marriage business gets done. The families of the fiancés get very happy.

Fake lovers look very good with each other. Princess with the white horses and the swans come together. In their external appearances, social ambitions, their attitude towards status, their deepest needs and their most hidden concerns, they evoke one another.

The confrontations in real love and the enrichment of love by these opposites are not seen in their so called relationship. All fake lovers have relationship. One night, casual or long term. For sex, for money, for status, for looks. For whatever reason. They all have relationships.

What you are at the beginning of a fake love, you're the same in the end. In true love, you become a different person. Real love changes a person permanently. Love is not a relationship. The basis of fake love is a dependency. Such lovers suck each other. They cling and absorb each other. They feed on each other.

Those relationships are boring while they are lived, disgusting when they end, and they never remembered. Some of those relationships never end up. They breakup and makeup. They split again. Then they can't stand alone without sex so jump on each other again. Suction continues. People who watch get mad. This cycle continues until one of the parties transfer to another fake love.

Real love in contrast, start with honour and end with honour. Fake lovers always talk about their love. They talk about the spell between each other. They always tell themselves "how good we are together!". Real lovers, however, never know the worth of each other. They live that magnificent time together as if it will never end. If it's not going to end, how could a beauty can always be remembered? Something you can spot cannot be a spell.

Fake loves are built on need, addiction and appreciation while true love is built on <u>lust and trust</u>.

Trust comes with absolute honesty, openness, authenticity, courage and the most important rule that you will never cheat on her.

How does lust come? This is something I never could understand. Being so hungry is not enough. Fucking her very well is even not enough. Forget about all the techniques. Maybe it's a gift from the gods. Maybe it is a destiny. Maybe something to do with the energy. Maybe that's why you can be the perfect lover for one woman and the worst loser for another.

Real love can defeat all enemies. Language, religion, race, class, culture differences, family and neighborhood pressures, everything. And they get married. Now there is only one obstacle in front of real love - time. Marriage is a great duel of love and time. Trust and lust live together in a house of drunks and insane.

Trust stays but lust wants to wander around. Because the lust's life is a lot shorter than trust. And it's an unstable weapon. He often jams. When the lust goes away couples get easily defeated. Most of the time in a year, a maximum of three years.

The purpose of nature is not happy marriages anyway. It's plenty of kids. That's why we suck at the beginning of a marriage. Nature doesn't care neither our happiness nor our marriage.

Define your success

If you choose to believe "success" with women is how many women you slept with, then although you will have quantity of experiences, all emotional quality will be lost, along with your happiness.

If you choose to believe "success" with women is how much money you can provide, then you will be be quite lonely followed by failure of your business.

If you choose to believe "success" with women is your looks, then get ready to lose her when someone who is better looking than you comes up.

If you choose to believe "success" with women is how alpha you are, then get ready to lose her when she finds out your beta parts.

<u>"You are what you believe"</u>.

If I were you, I would choose to believe "success" with women is in the <u>process</u> of finding the woman who makes you happy.

Forget about you giving her something or being someone. Forget about the end result and think about yourself. Define the success as the process of finding a woman or women who will maximize your happiness.

When you do that, instead of waiting and hoping for a woman to select you, you will start to screen as many women as possible until you find the one(s) you enjoy.

When you do that, instead of settling with a woman who no longer makes you happy, you will move on to find the one(s) who will make you happy.

On the way, you will find lots of sex, lot's of great experiences, and lot's, lots and lots of failures.

<u>But positives will always outweigh the negatives.</u>

Suddenly, you will understand that rejection helps your success rate. You will screen through these women by sharing your own truth with them openly. And when you do that, she will either become attracted to you or she will reject you.

Either way, you'll be happier for it because you won't be losing your <u>precious</u> time.

And maybe...you'll find real love in this process.

❊ ❊ ❊

Thank you for reading this book. I hope that it added at value and quality to your everyday life. If so, it would be really nice if you could shortly review it on Amazon. You can review it now using link https://www.amazon.com/dp/B0854NTZ4L

I wish you all the best in your future success!

Assignments

Approach 20 Women
Approach 20 women as I have written on day 1.

Write Your Daily Journal
Write your daily journal as I have written on day 1.

Manufactured by Amazon.ca
Acheson, AB